WAVES OF CHALLENGE

A History of
The Daytona Beach/Halifax Area

By
BROWARD LISTON

PARTNERS IN PROGRESS
by
Barbara Johnson

Taylor Publishing Company
Dallas

With The

Daytona Beach/Halifax Area
Chamber of Commerce

Waves of Challenge

A History of the Daytona Beach/Halifax Area

By Broward Liston

Partners in Progress by Barbara Johnson

Editors: Jeanne Warren Smith
Angie Miccinello

Photography Editor, James Tiller

Taylor Publishing Company
Dallas, Texas

David Danser, Publisher and Manager, Fine Books Division

John Galloway, Managing Editor

Barbara Johnson, Marketing Representative

Dust Jacket Design by Bonnie Henson, The Graphic Underground

Dust Jacket Photograph Courtesy of James Tiller

Book Design by Carolyn Horn, Designer, William Wilson & Associates

Published 1996
Printed in The United States of America
First Edition
Trade Edition ISBN Number: 0-87833-150-6

Dear Reader:

The Chamber, Daytona Beach/Halifax Area is proud to present *Waves of Challenge - The History of Daytona Beach/Halifax Area.* We feel that this publication is the most comprehensive history of our community ever written and covers its unique story, dating back 300 years.

To do this, The Chamber teamed up with Taylor Publishing Company, a national leader in its field, and award-winning author Brad Liston. Together we offer you, the reader, an exciting enjoyable read on the origins of Daytona Beach and the Halifax Area that takes you on a journey through the 1990's.

Waves of Challenge - The History of Daytona Beach/Halifax Area will be a "keepsake" for every family and will be treasured for years to come. We trust that you will enjoy reading it as much as we have enjoyed producing this fine historical text.

A special thanks to the task force who oversaw the production of this book: Walter Curtis, Dick Dunkel, Sarah Pappas and M.F. Warren. Their direction was invaluable.

Bill Olivari
Chairman of the Board

George Mirabal
President

City Island • P.O. Box 2475 • Daytona Beach, FL 32115-2475 • 904/255-0981

Photo: The Daytona Beach Pier during the days of the Florida Land Boom.

CONTENTS

*O*f *C*hallenge

Chapter 5: The Golden Age

From the war's end through the mid-60s, the Daytona Beach/Halifax area comes into its own. A mobile and thriving middle class takes to the highways and makes Daytona Beach its destination. Air conditioning is rare, so cool breezes along the Boardwalk and concerts in the Band Shell make Daytona the perfect place for "weekend vacations." Tourism booms. Home construction is strong and steady. Motels and tourist courts spring up along A1A. GI Bill veterans and their Baby Boom children account for new schools and colleges. Spring Break is born. And Bill France makes the new Daytona International Speedway a Mecca for race fans and an instant draw for the national media.

Chapter 6: Recession and Renaissance

In the '70s and '80s, the Daytona Beach/Halifax area faces the same hard problems most American cities must face. Added to that are changes in the tourism industry. Disney World takes people away from the beach, and the interstate highways take them further south. But civic leaders cushion the blow, and the seeds of a new renaissance are planted even as new problems mount. Daytona Beach never loses its idiosyncratic appeal. Bike Week brings potential troublemakers into the tent and makes them civic boosters. The Halifax River is cleaned up. And government gets involved in historic preservation and archaeology, spurring a renewed sense of community and involvement.

Chapter 7: Present and Future

A new era of cooperation between government and private enterprise is underway. Plans are made to give whole neighborhoods much needed face lifts. The area prepares for a new era of beach development, with a water park, hi-tech entertainment and family fun center all on the drawing boards.

Chapter 8: Partners in Progress

Profiles of leading companies and organizations chronicle the ongoing contributions of the business community to this vibrant region.

Chapter 1

Conquistadors To Civil War

God and Nation—1565

Jean Ribault, shipwrecked, hung over and on the run from cold-blooded killers, dragged his weary body from the surf that windy, wet September morning and took his first long look across the wide stretch of hard, silver sand. Beyond the sand was nothing but a thick forest of pine and palmetto. And beyond that, nothing but sky. History does not record his impressions of Daytona Beach, but that's understandable. Bad enough the King of Spain wanted him dead. At that particular moment, he was probably more worried about Indians than anything else.

Of course, Ribault, the senior French military officer in the New World of 1565, had no idea the beach where he landed would someday be called Daytona, or that his shipwreck was arguably the single most important event in Florida's history. Or, for that matter, that this disaster would have long-range implications for the United States of America, a nation that wouldn't exist for another two centuries.

If he didn't stop to ponder all the wonderful possibilities this wide stretch of beach offered, it's because he was supposed to be seventy miles north, attacking the tiny garrison of San Augustine that his nemesis, Pedro Menéndez de Avilés, had established just days before. But a sudden hurricane had ended that. It had also wrecked his entire fleet, and Ribault could now look back across the Atlantic Ocean and wonder just how he was supposed to cross the three thousand miles separating him from France.

His worries about Indians were not misplaced, either. The French were off to a bad start with these Indians, who called themselves something like Tomoka, or Timagoa, or Timucua, depending on how you heard their strange tongue. And Ribault couldn't be sure these bizarre natives, large and robust, who covered themselves in tattoos and sometimes wore whole stuffed animals for hats, weren't watching even now, preparing to come at his tiny party with stone battle axes and bows and arrows.

As it happened, the Indians were watching him. He'd wrecked near a large Timucuan village built along a trail that is today North Beach Street and ruled by a chief named Ostinola, whose influence spread over all the Indian villages along the Halifax River. These Frenchmen were the first white men to show their faces in his country, called *Toronita*, the Land of Sunshine. And whatever Ostinola and his warriors had heard of Europeans, it wouldn't have been good. But they did not attack, did not even show themselves. They stayed hidden in the forest and watched every

Left: Galleon ships off the coast of Florida. Both the French and Spanish sailed such fleets to Florida in the 16th century.

move made by Ribault and his comrades as they gathered on the beach. They watched and passed word of what they saw up the coast, where it eventually reached Menéndez at the garrison of San Augustine, who quickly set off in search of Ribault and his French survivors.

Right: A heavily romanticized depiction of Europeans arriving in the New World. The truth was often far scarier, as the story of Jean Ribault's arrival at Daytona Beach illustrates.

Ribault's story is filled with adventure and, ultimately, sadness. He'd come to Florida three years earlier to colonize it, and left behind a settlement on the St. Johns River, where Jacksonville is today. Another settlement was left on Paris Island, South Carolina, near Charleston. But Ribault was a Huguenot, a French Protestant who served a Catholic king, and when he returned to France for more colonists, he found himself embroiled in a religious war. He'd spent most of the intervening years in prison.

Admiral Ribault, like many who would follow him to North America, saw these shores as a potential haven from religious persecution. He also saw the New World as a land of opportunity for a man such as himself, with no aristocratic blood, who had worked his way up through the ranks of the French navy. In the Old World, land was wealth, and most of the land in France was owned by Catholics. This was new land. A fresh start. A new beginning.

Had Ribault succeeded, Florida's early history would be French rather than Spanish. And the French, who were far more aggressive colonizers than the Spanish, would have continued to spread their influence up the eastern seaboard, well ahead of English efforts at Jamestown and Plymouth Rock. Everything we know about American history would have been altered irrevocably. But history is written by the winners, as they say, and Ribault's chance to write it ended on Daytona Beach. More than four centuries later, in 1995, his descendants, some from France, some living in Atlanta, Georgia, came to Florida as tourists and were surprised to find that he figures so prominently in the state's history. There is a plaque in Daytona Beach marking the site of his shipwreck, a beachside street named for him, and even a high school bearing his name in Jacksonville. But in his own country he is virtually unknown. A mere footnote of failure.

Ribault's big problem was that the Spanish had already claimed Florida a half century before, when Juan Ponce de León, in the throes of a mid-life crisis, had set off on his quixotic search for the mythical Fountain of Youth. After that, the Spanish explored Florida haphazardly, hoping to find rich deposits of silver and gold. Failing to find either riches or magic, they mostly left it alone until Ribault and his compatriots began to colonize. That's when the King of Spain dispatched Menéndez, the governor of Puerto Rico and a ruthless warrior, with orders to "fortify the Florida coast, destroy the French and convert the Indians."

First, the Spanish established San Augustine as a small, armed camp, then marched north to attack the French settlement of Fort Caroline on the St. Johns River. They arrived after Ribault and his fleet had already set sail, and the Spanish not only sacked Fort Caroline, they slaughtered nearly all the two hundred women, children and elderly and infirm men whom Ribault had left behind. When word of the massacre reached Europe, Menéndez's name was permanently blackened everywhere but in Spain.

But it was not the destruction of Fort Caroline that doomed the French efforts, because Ribault had arrived at San Augustine to find it equally unguarded. What's more, Menéndez had left his entire fleet of warships behind when he opted for an overland march. Ribault could not believe his luck. He could easily rout the Spaniards from Florida by burning their fleet and taking Menéndez and his men captive when they returned. But the day was late, and the French did not want to stumble

around in the dark, so Ribault anchored his ships offshore and waited for dawn. That night, he and his officers celebrated their good fortune by drinking themselves silly, making a contest of it, goading one another on until each man had drunk about two gallons of wine.

That's when the storm hit. It was the first week of September, hurricane season, and the storm scattered the French fleet all down the coast, as far as Cape Canaveral. Not a single ship survived. With no way of knowing the fate of Fort Caroline, Ribault had no option but to gather as many of his men as he could—about four hundred—and set off in that direction.

He met up with Menéndez at the only inlet between Daytona Beach and San Augustine; Ribault's shipwrecked crew on the south shore, the heavily armed Spanish, who had arrived two days before, encamped to the north. Ribault crossed over with a few of his officers under a flag of truce. Menéndez had brought food and wine and they shared a very civilized meal, the first real food the Frenchmen had eaten in days. Then the Spaniard, seated by a campfire, calmly explained that there was no Fort Caroline for them to return to, omitting from the account his slaughter of the civilians. With no fort and no fleet, the French were stranded and Menéndez insisted on their unconditional surrender, but gave his assurances that Ribault and his men would be spared and returned to France. He required just one thing, that the French march back to San Augustine with their hands tied behind them. Menéndez said he simply couldn't risk having the French overwhelm his own guard. It was the best Ribault could hope for. He surrendered his sword, flag and gilded helmet and re-

The dunes at Matanzas Inlet. Spaniards from St. Augustine used these dunes to conceal their atrocities against the French.

crossed the bay to explain the terms to his countrymen. About half of them mistrusted the Spanish so much that they decided to take their chances with the Indians and mosquitoes and set off on foot. The rest were ferried ten at a time on a narrow bateau across the bay, their hands already bound.

Ribault was in the first group of ten to cross. On the shore, he and his nine companions were led to the far side of the dunes. There he met a sight that must have sickened him and made him curse the day he first set foot in Florida. Dozens of his countrymen who had arrived in a group a day ahead of him lay dead in piles, their hands tied behind them. Their heads were in another pile and their blood stained the white sand a deep red. Ribault would have felt rough hands forcing him to his knees then, and his last sensation a sword biting at his neck.

The story of Jean Ribault's shipwreck is important not only for what he and the French failed to do, but also for what the Spanish themselves failed to do. San Augustine, later St. Augustine, would go on to be fortified and settled, the oldest permanent European settlement in what is today the United States. But for the next two hundred years the Spanish viewed it as little more than the far-flung, northernmost outpost of their Caribbean colonies. Other European powers—the French, Dutch, and English—came to North America to colonize. They all built cities and developed agriculture to the north, leading to one of the seminal events in all of human history, the American Revolution. But while San Augustine stood its lonely guard, the rest of East Florida was not colonized in any meaningful way. The Spanish thought the soil too sandy, the underbrush too dense, the natural ports too far apart and the whole thing was just too plain close to the English to make them comfortable. They also had found the native Timucua too independent to enslave and too fierce to kill off.

Native Floridians

The Timucua were probably descendants of the first tribes to reach Florida 15,000 years ago, when the climate was cooler and drier and the shoreline about fifty miles to the east. These first Floridians hunted mastodons, giant ground sloths, ten-foot-long armadillos and other exotic fare vanished from today's menus, catching them at river fords as the animals were slowed by the water.

Like their early ancestors, the Timucua still hunted and warred with Stone Age arrows, spears and axes, and they continued to live along the rivers and coastlines, which suited their taste for game and shellfish. But the Timucua had a highly developed culture that would have been as frightening and mysterious to the first Floridians as our world of highways, high rises and hi-tech would be to the Timucua. They lived in villages and had complex social and political orders. They adorned their bodies with tattoos and jewelry. (Their jewelry included gold and silver mined thousands of miles away in Mexico and the American Southwest.) Their headgear was made of stuffed animals or beautifully woven feathers. Their lives revolved around elaborate rituals, especially their death rites. They were good farmers, expert astronomers, kept remarkably accurate calendars, and practiced medicine more advanced than the medical arts of Christopher Columbus's time. Technologically primitive but socially advanced.

The Timucua had been a stable society for more than two thousand years when Europeans first arrived. For perspective, that's about the same timespan separating us from Caesar and Cleopatra. Skeletons recovered from burial mounds show they often lived into their seventies, and males sometimes reached seven feet in height—both indicate good nutrition and low rates of disease.

MOUND
S BEACH ST
NEIGHBORHOOD WATCH
PROGRAM IN FORCE

Perhaps Ponce de León had found his Fountain of Youth without realizing it. But it wasn't some deepwater spring, filled with magic that rejuvenated you with a dip, it was a land of warm climates, fresh air and abundant food. The Timucua lived on seafood, root vegetables and berries, with occasional red meat—a good diet by today's standards and much better than the salted meats and oils the Europeans brought with them.

Top left: Turtle Mound, at the Canaveral National Seashore, is the highest natural point on Florida's east coast. The mound once stood 75 feet high, and for centuries navigators have used it as a reference point.

Bottom left: The smaller mound, just off South Beach Street in Ormond Beach, is one of the few remaining intact burial mounds.

There were some 10,000 natives in Florida when the Spanish arrived. Sadly, they were all but gone two hundred and fifty years later, when the Spanish departed. They could more than hold their own against the military might of Spain, but not their diseases. Measles, smallpox, typhoid and bubonic plague cut through them like a scythe. When the Spanish yielded Florida to the British in the 18th century, only a dozen or so Timucuans survived, and they had grown so dependent on Spanish missionaries that they could no longer live off the land, so they boarded the Spanish ships and disappeared into history.

Despite their own long history, most of what we know of the Timucua comes from archaeologists and anthropologists. The Timucuans left no written records. But they did leave behind ample evidence of themselves in their garbage. Throughout the Halifax area the Timucua left large garbage mounds, called middens, where they discarded shells, broken pottery and weapons, and bones from fish and game. These were nothing more than garbage dumps to the Timucua, but rich sources for today's archeologists. Their very size—at least one midden, Turtle Mound, reached a height of seventy-five feet—shows that village life was stable. The Timucuan diet was heavily weighted toward shellfish and other seafood, and when they did eat red meat it was roasted over pits.

The word "barbecue" probably comes to us from the Timucua as corrupted by the Spanish and French who saw whole goats being roasted over those open pits. To them, the Timucuan word sounded very much as if they were roasting the goats from "beard to tail" or *barbe en quayle*.

A remarkable account of the Timucua was written by a young man named Ernst d'Erlach, one of Ribault's crew who refused to surrender at Matanzas Inlet. He and the others set off to find their wrecked ships, hoping to recover enough timber to build a single ship capable of returning them to France. But they did not retrace their route along the open beach, fearful that Menéndez would pursue them that way. Instead they followed the Halifax River, taking them directly through a number of Timucuan villages. They found the natives friendly and helpful beyond all their expectations. Certainly these weary stragglers posed no threat to the Timucua, and it may also be the Indians were outraged by Menéndez's slaughter.

In any case, d'Erlach lived among the Timucua for a time at what is today Ormond Beach, and even married a daughter of Chief Ostinola—the first Christian wedding performed in Volusia County. Otherwise little is known of d'Erlach, except that he was eventually rescued by a French ship searching for survivors. His account of the Timucua in Volusia County is a bit romanticized in parts—this was, after all, long before anthropology became a discipline—but it is also the only written account of the Halifax natives before the influence of Europe.

D'Erlach wrote:

> *Their features are fine and regular. Their foreheads high, their eyes lustrous, their countenances full of spirit and their manners so pleasing—not to be excelled by the best gentlemen of France—that it is good to be in their company.*

The recreation of a Timucuan village. The Timucua Indians lived in similar villages for about 2,000 years before they were all but wiped out by European diseases. Grass mats were used to enclose the thatched huts during winter months.

> *Their garments, although somewhat scanty, set forth their figures well and leave them perfect freedom of motion. They wear a tunic around their loins, leggings and moccasins to keep their feet and legs from being torn apart by thorns and brambles; cloaks of grass cloth, skins and sometimes feathers woven together, but with little difference between the sexes. . . It is a marvel to see how little the sun or wind or rain does affect their bodies, when yet the stoutest of us would perish if we went about in like manner.*

D'Erlach describes the Timucua as matchless bow hunters, firing arrows so quickly that the first would still be in air when the second was strung and fired. They hit birds on the wing and even matched Robin Hood's trick of splitting an arrow at twenty paces.

He also wrote about their religious beliefs.

French artist Jacques le Moyne produced these 16th century pictures of Timucua Indians. At left, a slightly romanticized depiction of an alligator hunt. The picture below probably depicts fishing, though there is some possibility that le Moyne was suggesting that the Timucua mined gold from Florida's waters. They didn't, but false claims of New World gold were often used to raise money for future expeditions.

> *They have no idols or temples, for their God is a Great Spirit, whose dwelling is the universe, who is always near them, although invisible; to whom they pray in times of tribulation; who sometimes answers them not. But there are many lesser spirits, some good, some bad, whose favor they seek in hunting, fishing, love and war.*

D'Erlach watched the women make pottery from clay found along the river shore, some jars large enough to store grain, others small enough to hold their makeup. He

Below: A conquistador's helmet on display at the Halifax Historical Society Museum on South Beach Street.

Right: Three Timucuan figures from a sculpture by Fred Dean Marsh at Tomoka State Park.

stayed in their homes, which were circular and dome-shaped. The roofs were palmetto-thatched, the walls built by driving posts into the ground and wrapping them with palmetto matting that could be taken down in the warmer months. Inside were wooden benches for sitting and sleeping. Each village was dominated by a large, central community house. The chief and his family lived there, but it was also used for religious ceremonies and political gatherings. Nearby was the armory. Surrounding them were smaller family homes.

No doubt d'Erlach also visited their charnel houses, where the dead were prepared for burial, the bodies stretched out on long racks. Every day the priests would come and peel away the flesh as it decayed, until the bodies were clean to the bone. Then the bones would be bundled and buried side by side in sand mounds, as many as a hundred bodies to a mound, often with the deceased's most prized possessions.

In the late 19th and early 20th centuries, many of the burial mounds, as well as the garbage dumps, where dug up by the railroads and road construction crews for use as fill. The bones were often found perfectly preserved, though they began to crumble when exposed to air. Like Egyptian mummies, which used to be ground up for medicines and aphrodisiacs, their potential value simply wasn't estimated. Unfortunately, we probably will never know as much about the Timucuans as we do the Egyptians and other ancient people. Why they buried their dead as they did, how they envisioned the afterlife and many other aspects of their culture may be lost forever. We have very little idea of how they saw themselves; we only know how they were seen by outsiders who could not begin to understand them fully.

More dependable, and much more familiar, are d'Erlach's descriptions of the natural surroundings, *"a scene of matchless beauty—yet soft and pleasant beauty, not the beauty of majesty. . .for unlike other lands, there are no high mountains or rugged cliffs and precipices."* He saw the many sand bars of the Halifax and islands white with herons, oyster reefs in the inlet and waters that *"abound in oysters and fish, also large turtles, caught often by the natives sleeping on the surface of the water, they being excellent for food."*

D'Erlach's highest praise was reserved for the beach, which he describes as *"one of the finest in the world, hard and broad enough to march a large army over it in ranked battalions. And though the sun might shine ever so brightly, moist with the tides and cooled by the sea winds, it is seldom hot or uncomfortable."*

Remarkably, this first written account of the Halifax holds up pretty well more than four hundred years later. The armies crossing the beach today are sunbathers, and the soft and gentle lands yield a fair number of golf courses. And many natives still sport tattoos and don't wear a lot of clothes. But d'Erlach's praise did little to promote Florida. Europeans were still two hundred years away from settling the Halifax. In the meantime, the Spanish would do little more than use its mouth—today called Ponce de León Inlet, but for most of its history known as Mosquito Inlet—to launch pirating raids against British merchant ships moving between the northern colonies and the West Indies.

Historians have long been baffled as to why the Spaniards remained blind to the area's potential. They had only to look to the Indians to see what Florida could, and someday would, become. The Timucua used strong timber to build their boats, grew indigo for dye, harvested cane, and hunted and fished. They lived quite well off the land, and, until disease took them in large numbers, they lived long and happy lives. In the years to come, the Halifax would support whole industries devoted to those same pursuits. Meanwhile, the Spaniards in San Augustine rarely ventured far beyond its walls. They sent home for even the simplest supplies and never developed the skills to make do for themselves. In hard times, they simply raided the Indians for what they needed. It would be left to the British to develop the Halifax region. But that is a story that is rarely inspiring, as their means were often the most brutal available.

Chapter 2

Cities, Railroads, And The Idle Rich

The Failure of Civilization

James Grant was a tireless promoter of Florida, forever praising the beaches and climate, the cheap land and the bounty of natural resources. He began in 1764, just one year after England emerged the big winner in the Seven Years' War, claiming Florida and all of Canada as her prizes.

Grant had been a redcoat general on the American frontier, where the fighting had been called the French and Indian War. He'd spent much of his career in North America and understood the peculiar way frontier life mixed with European culture in the colonies. That made him a good choice to be King George III's first colonial governor of Florida, which was all frontier and very little culture. It was Grant's job to bring this new colony into the fold, to make it the equal of older colonies to the north. He concentrated his effort on the east coast, from the St. Marys River in the north, to New Smyrna, an area that included all of the Halifax. West Florida, meanwhile, would become a separate colony with its capital in Pensacola.

Grant was hard at work as soon as he debarked in the newly Anglicized capital of St. Augustine, issuing proclamations, writing letters to the editors of English language-periodicals, not even taking time for the elaborate ceremonies that usually marked the arrival of a new governor. He extolled the sunny climate for its healthful qualities, touted the soil and moisture as perfect for indigo and tropical fruits, and boasted to shipbuilders of live oaks that took a day to saw through.

A road system, called the King's Road, was planned and begun. Grant gave the Halifax River its name, honoring George Mantagu Dunk, Earl of Halifax and a close political ally of the king, perhaps thinking the Spanish name, Rio Mosquito, insufficiently enticing. He helped the Scotsman Andrew Turnbull, a successful London physician, put together funding for a colony at New Smyrna, named for the birthplace of Turnbull's Greek wife. He paid to relocate forty families of artisans from Bermuda to what is now Volusia County. And he rewarded war veterans with generous grants. Field officers were entitled to five thousand acres, staff officers got two thousand, noncommissioned officers two hundred and fifty, and privates fifty. He also persuaded plantation families in Georgia and South Carolina to send their noninheriting sons to expand the family fortunes with new plantations in Florida.

Left: The unspoiled beauty of the Halifax area, much as the English found it when they began to develop plantations there.

And he brought slaves from Africa by the thousands, as many as five hundred to a ship, to become the muscle and bone of the colonial effort, transforming the wilderness into fields of sugar cane and hemp, or irrigating them for rice.

An 18th-century silhouette of Andrew Turnbull, founder of the New Smyrna colony.

But for all his effort, Grant never succeeded in making Florida a thriving colony. The British gentry undermined him, staking out immense plantations, usually measuring into the tens of thousands of acres. These plantations, such as Mount Oswald, built by Richard Oswald at the head of the Halifax River, and the estate of James Moultrie near the mouth of the Tomoka River, were so large that there was no room for towns and villages to spring up naturally.

That made life difficult for the smaller landowners, who had to travel all the way to St. Augustine for supplies. It also doomed the Turnbull Colony. Turnbull had brought Greek, Minorcan and Italian immigrants to his colony as indentured workers, promising them their own land at the close of their contracts. But the experiment ended so badly that Turnbull was later accused of enslaving the immigrants, starving them and working many of them to death. A group escaped to St. Augustine and appealed to Grant's political enemies for help. All of the immigrants were later relocated to St. Augustine, where the Minorcan stonemasons and their descendants were to build much of the city's most distinctive architecture.

It didn't help matters that the largest landowners, such as Oswald, lived in England, or, like Moultrie, in St. Augustine. They rarely, if ever, lived on their own plantations. Such men became known as "Florida monopolists" in the British press, and formed the backbone of opposition to Grant's efforts to increase Florida's population.

Plantation life in Florida was different than in the other southern colonies. There was none of the plantation society found in older colonies, such as Virginia, where the deep association of families with names like Washington, Jefferson and Lee to their homelands was a contributing factor to the American Revolution and later the Civil War. So there was never any real possibility that Florida would break away with its thirteen northern neighbors in 1776.

But the American Revolution did bring a quick end to the British occupation of Florida. The newly emergent United States of America was understandably edgy about having a base for British military operations so near its borders. Ironically, it was Richard Oswald, owner of Mount Oswald and a friend and admirer of Benjamin Franklin, who helped negotiate the return of Florida to Spain at the Paris treaty talks.

Thus, the British history of Florida and the Halifax area ended after just two decades, and as quickly as it started. Most Floridians did not even know their home was a bargaining chip in treaty talks until the treaty was signed in 1783. Spain immediately ordered non-Spaniards out. For many, the news was devastating. Many of the families from Georgia and South Carolina had abandoned their property in those states during the Revolution so they could live in Florida and remain loyal to George III. And the smaller Florida plantations had not been up and running long enough to make themselves profitable, so there was little real wealth among the stranded landowners. Now they were essentially homeless. England had acquired the somewhat barren Bahamas from Spain in exchange, and many Floridians headed there. Others sailed for Nova Scotia. Some simply returned to England, regardless of their prospects.

But the dislocation of white residents, though severe, was nothing compared to the trauma experienced by blacks. Returning to Africa was not an option, of course, nor was following their owners to England or Nova Scotia, where slavery was banned. Some were freed, but the great majority wound up on the block, their owners willing to take bottom dollar on the suddenly glutted slave market in order to scrape a little money together for themselves. On a scale rarely seen, whole families were torn apart, husbands from wives, children from parents, most of them never to see one another again.

The Spanish began to administer Florida much as they had before, which is to say hardly at all. They opened the state to Spanish colonization, but no one came, and after three years it was hard to tell there had ever been working plantations on the Halifax. The fields were quickly covered in underbrush, while earthen irrigation systems crumbled. The wooden farm buildings were burned or blown away by storms, and nothing was left of the great coquina houses but their shells. None of that should imply that the Spanish were merely indolent. The simple fact was that they were broke. Spanish imperialism was about to run out its string, and investors were naturally wary of Florida after the horrendous experience of the British.

There was also a new worry for colonizers. Starting about 1750, a breakaway tribe of Creek Indians had begun to wander down from Georgia and Alabama. In fact, they would take their name from the Creek word for wanderer—Seminole. The Creek had allied themselves with the British during the Revolutionary War and kept

A plaque marking Old King's Road in Daytona Beach. Sections of Florida's oldest highway, built by English colonialists in the 18th century, are still in use today.

up their contacts even after the war. That made the Spanish especially leery. And their fears were borne out when the Seminoles began raids against the few manned outposts along the St. Johns River. For the most part, Spanish officials holed themselves up in St. Augustine and rarely ventured beyond the city's walls.

Then, in 1787, the Spanish opened Florida to non-Spanish immigration, and Florida's second plantation period was underway. A new generation of plantation owners arrived. The Spanish subdivided the mammoth estates of the English gentry to make them affordable to men with less wealth. These became the Spanish Land Grants by which much of the property in Florida is still divided. Englishmen and Scots poured into the state, with many settling along the Halifax. Again, some followed from the Carolinas and Georgia, and by 1803 most of the land along the Halifax had been granted.

Familiar names made their way to the Halifax. James Ormond, a Scotsman, arrived from the Bahamas. Charles W. Bulow came from South Carolina. And then there was the grant to Samuel Williams. Williams would play no great part in the area's history, but his land would. One day it would form the original city limits of Daytona.

These were prosperous days. The billowing white sails of merchant ships crisscrossed the horizon, moving cotton and sugar, indigo and corn to factories, refineries and mills in the north, and returning with the wealth of the world. For the only time in its history, the eastern coast of today's Volusia County was the richest land in Florida. But it proved to be a very short time.

Deep within Florida's interior, the Seminole nation nursed a horrible anger. Before coming to Florida, the Seminoles had been part of a nation, the Creek Indians, second only to the Cherokee east of the Mississippi. Now they were cut off from their brother Creeks by development along the Florida-Georgia border. The Seminoles were feeling squeezed, especially when plantations sprang up west of the St. Johns.

Despite their name, the Seminoles were not really wanderers. They built permanent villages of log houses with plaster walls along rivers and creeks—hence their original name, Creek Indians. The women cultivated fields of corn, squash, beans and other crops, and the men hunted, fished and even herded cattle. But the plantation owners routinely dammed the waterways for irrigation, and overnight an entire village could find itself homeless and on the move.

The Seminoles retaliated by taking in runaway slaves, which only encouraged more runaways and the violent reaction of slave owners. Ormond, the Scotsman whose name would spread around the world as Ormond Beach and the Ormond Hotel garnered fame, was killed while pursuing a runaway slave across the Spruce Creek plantation.

Spain's administration over East and West Florida was weak, essentially hands-off, so the Seminoles got no relief from St. Augustine or Pensacola. In the War of 1812, they again sided with the British, hoping the redcoats would take over Florida and sign a treaty with them. But the war ended with Florida still in Spanish hands,

Another picture of pristine beauty in the Halifax area.

so the Seminoles began making raids across the border into Georgia. That brought a swift and forceful response from the United States. General Andrew Jackson swept into Florida, attacked the Seminoles, then went on to seize Pensacola from the Spanish, bringing West Florida directly under U.S. control. Soon after, Spain sold East Florida to the United States for $5 million, and Jackson was appointed governor of the newly reunited territory. That only made matters worse for the Seminoles. Jackson flooded the state with colonists, pushing the Indians deeper into Florida's swampy south, where they could no longer grow crops.

The fuse had been lit, and when the Seminoles exploded, it would mean the end of prosperity and plantation life on the Halifax.

Seminole Rage

James Ormond III, grandson of the Ormond killed by a runaway slave, was a prosperous old man in 1892, a pillar of his community, so stately and so. . . well. . .old, that it was hard to picture him running through the wilds of East Florida

fighting Indians as a young man. Certainly his grandchildren couldn't picture him doing any such thing. But it had been an important time, personally. For him, home would always be Damietta, the plantation he'd come to as a boy of eight from Scotland. The same home he'd fought a war to protect, and lost. He'd been wounded four times in the only real battle ever waged in his home county, unless you count the Yankee shelling of nearly abandoned New Smyrna in the War Between the States. So he sat down and wrote out a memoir so his children and grandchildren would know him better. Also, so they and others would know their own history a little better. Over the years, so many tales had been told about the Battle of Dun-Lawton that a person might think Gettysburg had been fought there. James Ormond liked a good tale, too, but his memoirs were straightforward, tinged more with regret than pride.

Right: In a modern recreation of the Battle of Dun-Lawton, a Mosquito Roarer fires his rifle.

In 1835, Ormond joined the Mosquito Roarers, a militia brigade under the command of U.S. Army Major Benjamin A. Putnam. *"The whole company was just an undisciplined rabble, under no command of their officers,"* Ormond wrote. *"Not a man had ever seen a gun fired in anger."* By this time the Second Seminole War, as it came to be known, was already in high gear. More than a decade earlier, the Seminoles had agreed to leave the northern areas of the state, moving south of an imaginary line drawn twenty miles below Micanopy. White plantation owners were not supposed to develop the state's interior below that mark. But then the Seminoles' old enemy, Andy Jackson, was elected President of the United States, and he wanted the Seminoles, and every other Indian tribe in the southeast, relocated west of the Mississippi River. Federal Indian agents worked out a financial settlement with the seven Seminole chiefs that would have paid them more than $45,000 over ten years once they relocated to Arkansas. But the chiefs could not sell the plan to their villages, especially to younger men such as Osceola, Billy Bow Legs and Coacoochee, who became the real political powers in the Seminole nation. Suddenly, the younger men found themselves leading a people ready for war. The Seminoles rejected all their previous deals with the federal government. Federal troops were dispatched to Florida and the infamous Dade Massacre at the hands of Osceola marked the start of general warfare.

Fighting drove many of the Indians from the interior toward the coastal regions. Many settled in the wetlands of the Tomoka, where they could launch raids at will, then disappear back into the swampy forests. Already, sixteen plantations, each employing as many as four hundred slaves, had been abandoned between New Smyrna and the Matanzas Inlet.

Putnam and his militia had been ordered to take control of the Tomoka area and had set up headquarters at Bulowville, the home of John J. Bulow, Jr. and the most prosperous Plantation in Florida. Following reports that a large Indian party had made camp at the Dun-Lawton plantation, owned by John George Anderson, Putnam and his brigade set off down the Halifax River in a flotilla of small boats until they were opposite Anderson's property. It is here that we pick up Ormond's narration, as he and the other Roarers get their first glimpse of Seminole handiwork.

> *The houses were still on fire—that is, the dwellings along the riverbank. The mills were a mile or more back from the river. The first thing we in our boats saw was that some of our men had gone ashore and were chasing chickens around the burning houses. The Seminoles had penned up all the cattle and made their camp near the mills, apparently planning to drive off the cattle the next morning.*

Ormond and his fellow Roarers took up their position between the cattle pens and the Seminole camp and waited for sunrise.

Soon after daylight a single Indian warrior was seen coming down the road towards the pen, and as soon as he got within range they opened fire on the poor fellow and he was soon a corpse. Some of our brutes mutilated it shamefully.

Right: An old trail on the Bulow Plantation.

The militia's ambush had failed, wasted on a single Seminole warrior. The gunfire was enough to alert the main body of Seminoles, so Putnam's brigade fell back to the riverbank where they could find some shelter in the ruins of the burned houses.

Soon, the whole band of Indians, headed by Coacoochee, or, as he was known by the settlers, 'Wild Cat,'. . .mounted on a white or gray horse, in full war paint and costume, and with the reflectors from the Mosquito Bar Lighthouse, which they had burned a few days before, as a head ornament, came charging down upon us. The Indians had the advantage of us from the first, as they had scrub to hide in and shoot from, while we were mostly in the open. After firing at one another for, I suppose, half an hour or so, we were ordered to retreat to our boats.

It's worth noting that both sides were firing away at each other with old muzzle-loaded flintlock rifles. They were cumbersome, difficult to load and hard to aim, so a half hour of fighting might involve each man firing no more than a dozen or so times. But the lead miniballs whizzing through the air could be more deadly than a modern, jacketed bullet, which is designed to pass right through the body. The balls tended to splatter when they hit bone. Wounds were messy and hard to treat. Men tended to bleed to death internally when shot, or die from infections weeks, months, even years later.

Ormond wrote that the Roarers' retreat *"was done in some haste.". . .some of the party was left behind. 'Old Ben,' (Ben Wiggins) our old mulatto guide and interpreter, was greatly scandalized at the move and called out: 'My God, gentlemen, is you-uns going to run from a passle of damned Indians?' Major Putnam, seeing the effect of his stupid order to retreat, called to the men, who I am glad to say, responded gallantly, resuming the fight. . . .*

But once again, the Roarers failed to send the Seminoles running, so Putnam ordered a second retreat.

"This was a most distressing order," Ormond wrote. *"At the first order to retreat, as I said, some of the men were left behind. Now, the tide was out, our boats a good way out in the shallow water."* And it was soon every man for himself, running through the shallows to get to the boats, many of them dragging their guns through the water or splashing water all over the flintlocks, making them impossible to fire.

Our largest boat, a whale boat, was hard and fast aground and in the hurry was left behind. One man only, up to this time, had been killed on the spot—Will, a good black waiting man belonging to John George Anderson.

Right: Coacoochee, the Seminole leader who won the battle of Dun-Lawton.

> *The Indians got the whale boat afloat and while those on shore kept up a fire on us, a party of them had the boldness to follow us out into the river. After a while, one gun was got in order to shoot again and as the whale boat. . . approached us, a lucky shot ricocheting along the water keeled over one of the braves and he toppled into the water and they turned back.*
>
> *In the meantime, two of our party, Ned Gould and George Marks, both of St. Augustine, got so badly scared that they would not get into the boats, but ran on a dry spit of sand that led to Pelican Island. Marks swam the river and got to Camp Bulow about as soon as we did, but poor Gould, afraid to try it, was captured by the Indians and dreadfully tortured, so we learned afterwards.*

Ormond was shot four times. Once through the ear, again through the right shoulder and in the right wrist. But the worst was a bullet in the left side that lodged along the spine and had to be removed by a surgeon.

"So ended the Battle of Dun-Lawton, in which we were completely whipped by the Indians, and no doubt about it."

It is interesting to note that most of the slaves along the Halifax were sent to St. Augustine during this period. Many blacks had formed close attachments among the Indians, often intermarrying, and the slave owners worried about a black uprising if the slaves were able to see how effectively the Seminoles terrorized the countryside. The point was largely academic though, since the Seminoles eventually put all the Halifax plantations to the torch. That same year, a record freeze ruined most of the remaining agriculture in eastern Florida. The plantations never recovered.

Eventually, President Jackson would order the U.S. Army, under the command of Maj. Gen. Winfield Scott, to engage the Seminoles. But the army had no more success than the Mosquito Roarers. The war dragged on, with neither side gaining any real tactical advantage until 1845, proving very costly for the United States, as much in human life as in currency. But the Seminoles finally decided the war was unwinnable. Most had grown weary of fighting and reluctantly agreed to resettlement in Oklahoma and Arkansas. Several hundred fled into the Everglades, and it is their descendants who live on the modern Seminole reservations in Florida.

Among those to relocate was Coacoochee, the victor at Dun-Lawton and commander of the Seminole forces east of the St. Johns River. Coacoochee was born and raised in what is today southwestern Volusia County. As the son of a chief, it was not uncommon for him to mix socially with many of the families he would later burn out of their homes. He was a man of piquant humor, his attitude toward women quite gallant and toward children very kindly, all of which made him a popular dinner guest before the war. He was known to move white men to tears with the story of his twin sister's early death and his own belief that she acted as a spirit guide to him throughout his life. But the refinement of his wit and manners belied a deep sense of wrong that worried all Seminoles like an open wound. As he was waiting in chains in Tampa to be carried by ship into exile, he gave this account of his relationship with the white man:

> *When I was a boy. . .I saw the white man afar off. I hunted in these woods, first with a bow and arrow, then with a rifle. I saw the white man, and was told that he was my enemy. I could*

An exaggerated and highly romanticized depiction of fighting during the Second Seminole War, which brought an end to the plantation era on the Halifax.

not shoot him as I would a wolf or a bear, yet like these he came upon me. Horses, cattle and fields he took from me. He said he was my friend; he abused our women and children and told us to go from the land. Still, he gave me his hand in friendship; we took it; whilst taking it, he had a snake in the other. . . he lied, and stung us. I asked him but for a small piece of these lands, enough to plant and live upon, far south, a spot where I could place the ashes of my kindred, a spot only sufficient upon which I could lay my wife and child. This was not granted me. . . . It is true I have fought like a man, so have my warriors; but the whites are too strong for us.

Coacoochee had been captured in 1837 with Osceola and imprisoned in Fort Marion. He starved himself until he was thin enough to squeeze through the iron bars of his cell and escape, even though it meant tearing the skin from his back and chest as he forced himself out. Though he would eventually surrender again, the fight never left him. As an old man he grew restless in Arkansas, where the Seminoles had been thrown in with Creek Indians and placed under the leadership of their tribal council. Coacoochee and several hundred Seminoles escaped to Mexico, where they founded their own village in the Santa Rosa Mountains, and he remained there until his death.

Once the Indian issue had been settled in Florida, Congress quickly granted the territory statehood in 1845, but the Halifax area would be left largely abandoned until after the Civil War, except for a few timber and turpentine camps. The hard wood of the live oak tree was still valued for shipbuilding, but the camps were seasonal and never developed into communities.

In the western county, along the St. Johns River, with its access to the port at Jacksonville, settlers began to return by 1854. That was the same year the legislature established Volusia County, which stretched from Matanzas Inlet to below Cape Canaveral. In that year, there were thirty-eight families in the entire county. It was scarred country, scarred by the Seminoles, but also by the federal troops that had occupied it, seizing homes, boats, wagons, crops and slaves at will. Resentment was still there in 1861 when Florida left the Union and joined the Confederacy, and it accounts for some of the enthusiasm felt for secession at the time. But there were to be no great battles fought along the Halifax. The Civil War was just one more thing in the area's history that kept anyone from making a real go of it in eastern Volusia. This time it was the Union naval blockade that choked off commerce through Mosquito Inlet, today called Ponce de León Inlet, and the Union occupation of Jacksonville and St. Augustine to the north. Both the Halifax and St. Johns Rivers would be bottled up throughout the war. Confederate blockade runners did make it through to Mosquito Inlet, but the munitions and supplies, most of them from Great Britain, were destined for an overland route to Waldo in Alachua County, where Confederate trains would take them to Atlanta for redistribution to armies in the field.

To this point, the area's history had been colorful but largely marked by failure. At the close of the Civil War, with the Halifax area in ruin for decades, few would have believed that a century of success was just around the corner. But it was. One of the world's great destinations was about to be discovered.

The sugar mill at Dun-Lawton plantation (above and left), burned by Seminoles shortly before the battle fought there.

The ruins of Bulowville, the plantation where the Mosquito Roarers were headquartered.

Camp
Hope

Chapter 3

Boom and Bust

New Beginnings

Mathias Day, a pious, middle-aged Ohioan from a well-to-do family, was shopping for real estate in Florida when he met a big Swede with coarse hands named John Andrew Bostrom. Day was well educated, politically connected and had prospered at everything he set his hand to—newspaper publisher, manufacturer, inventor. Bostrom, on the other hand, had been raised on a farm, then wandered the world doing odd jobs—fisherman, merchant seaman, store clerk and, now, citrus grower. His goal was to scrape together enough money to marry his sweetheart and bring her to Florida.

The two men had little in common except that each was an icon of his times—Day, the wealthy industrialist, for whom success fit as neatly as a tailored waistcoat, and Bostrom, the hard-working immigrant who knew that a broad back, a clear head and all the endurance of Atlas could punch his ticket to a better future. As it turned out, their meeting in 1870 was to be the seminal event in the history of the Halifax area.

Palmetto-thatched cabins like the one at left were home to many Halifax pioneers when settlers arrived after the Civil War.

Below: Mathias Day, inventor, publisher, industrialist and founder of the city of Daytona, pictured about the time he came to Florida.

Bostrom had arrived in Florida in 1865 just after the Civil War. He'd met up with a man named John Mollison in St. Augustine. The two set off to explore Florida's east coast, looking for good land to start orange groves. When they arrived on the Halifax, they had as their guide a freed slave named Israel McKinney, who showed them the ruins of old plantations where he'd once worked. The two white men became interested in a piece of beachside land that McKinney called "Hog Pen," across the river from the old Williams plantation. Bostrom and Mollison settled on Hog Pen, but not before Bostrom rechristened it Sylvan Beach, though most people who heard his foreign accent thought he was saying "Silver Beach," the name it is known by today. Bostrom sent to Sweden for his brother, Charles, and with Mollison they began to develop the land for orange groves. It wasn't long though, before the partners had a falling out over management of the property. The Bostrom brothers took land further north, beachside property across the river from the old Henry Yonge plantation. They hammered together a palmetto shack, planted their trees, then started to earn a meager living as boat builders as their groves matured. Later they built a small two-story home using bricks from old plantation homes and timber and shingles salvaged from shipwrecks. It was said that Charles Bostrom, or Charley as he became known in America, could tear apart a foundered ship faster than any man on the coast. Once their new home was built, they began to take in an occasional boarder.

Florida was hardly a tourist mecca in those days, but with the war's end, people began heading there in the winters, often at a doctor's suggestion.

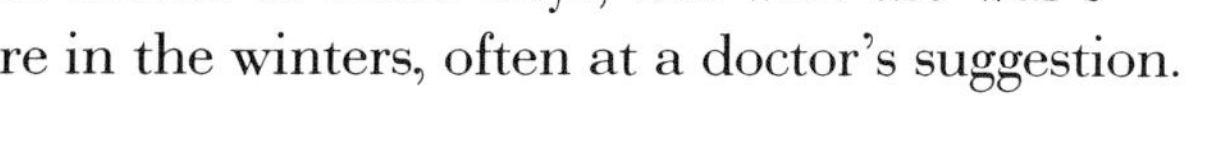

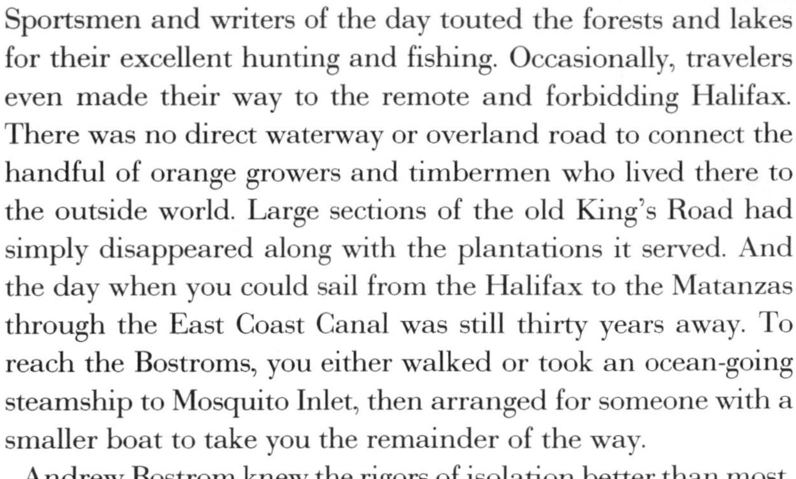

Sportsmen and writers of the day touted the forests and lakes for their excellent hunting and fishing. Occasionally, travelers even made their way to the remote and forbidding Halifax. There was no direct waterway or overland road to connect the handful of orange growers and timbermen who lived there to the outside world. Large sections of the old King's Road had simply disappeared along with the plantations it served. And the day when you could sail from the Halifax to the Matanzas through the East Coast Canal was still thirty years away. To reach the Bostroms, you either walked or took an ocean-going steamship to Mosquito Inlet, then arranged for someone with a smaller boat to take you the remainder of the way.

Andrew Bostrom knew the rigors of isolation better than most. When he served on the Volusia County Board of Commissioners in 1868, he had to sail his boat down river to Port Orange, which was little more than a post office in those days, then walk thirty miles to Enterprise, the county seat. Along the way he crossed several creeks and streams and, if the water was high, had to tie his clothes to his head and swim across. The trip took two days.

Above: Until the railroads arrived, Daytona and Ormond were deeply isolated from the rest of the world. A scene like the one above might be a romantic interlude, or the beginning of an arduous three day trip to Jacksonville.

Below: Small sail boats were vital to the early communities of Daytona and Ormond. They were the fastest way to move up and down the river, but they were scarce.

Day's Town

In the spring of 1870, Bostrom traveled to Jacksonville with another man, John Hawks, for supplies. There they heard about Mathias Day and introduced themselves. It's likely that neither Bostrom nor Day understood how auspicious their meeting would be. Bostrom invited Day to stay with him and look over other property on the Halifax, but Day first sailed with Hawks for the Indian River, then known as the Hillsborough River, and inspected land south of New Smyrna. He wasn't happy with what he saw, so he stopped over at Bostrom's on his return voyage.

Day was impressed by the Bostroms' hospitality, their easy-going manner and good humor. He inspected their budding groves and the brothers took him exploring. That evening, as he would later write, he was *"treated to a splendid supper put up by Helen Bostrom,"* a sister, who along with another sister, Mary, had arrived from Sweden to join their brothers. And that night he slept on a bed he would describe as the best he ever slept on in Florida.

The next morning, bright and early, he struck off by himself for the beach, walking a half mile down the path his hosts had cleared through the brush and dunes. The beach was a fine place to watch the early sun climb the sky. Day could look to his right or left and see the broad stretch of hard, flat sand stretching straight away for miles, like a grand and glorious boulevard. He began to walk and his shoes barely sank in the sand as he stepped briskly along. It was a fine, mild April morning and he had the beach all to himself. The waves swelled and rolled so invitingly that Day stripped off his clothes, quick as a young Tom Sawyer, and plunged in, shouting hymns and hallelujahs, throwing up his arms and letting the waves crash over him. He felt young again. It was like falling in love, and he would write in his diary that this beach was *"doubtless the finest on the U.S. continent, where a man can have a thirty-mile trot on hard sand*

This early photograph of South Beach Street in Daytona Beach shows the town just as Mathias Day envisioned it, with wide, tree-lined streets and large lots, the homes set forward, near the street.

William Jackson's General Store was one of the first businesses to open in the Halifax area.

floor, perfectly smooth. Surf and sea air invigorating and refreshing. I shucked myself and plunged in and said, 'Roll on thou deep and dark blue ocean, roll . . . and she rolled.' "

Later that morning, after a breakfast of hominy and eggs, Andrew Bostrom took Day aboard his small sailboat and the two men made their way six miles down the Halifax, past alligators, leaping mullet and live oak trees dripping their Spanish moss to the water. They stopped at the Samuel Williams grant, twelve miles north of the inlet. In the thirty-five years since Samuel Hill Williams had hid in the trees and watched Seminoles burn his house and fields, the land had been covered by a new growth of oak, hickory, pine, palmetto and mulberry. This fertile hammock stretched west about four miles. Perfect for the groves Day envisioned, and perfect for the town they would support. He left the Bostroms, took a steamship to St. Augustine, tracked down the current owners of the Williams property and bought it for $1,200 down and an $8,000 mortgage.

Day probably was not the greatest visionary to ever stride along the Halifax, but he was a visionary nonetheless, who saw more than cheap land in a good climate. Day had been schooled at Oberlin College, steeped in the evangelical Calvinism of Charles Grandison Finney. Day believed, as many did in those times, that a good Christian was God's instrument for making a better world, and those whom God chose, he often made wealthy, so they'd have the resources to do his work. That faith had made him an active abolitionist before the Civil War and a successful businessman since. He firmly believed in the limitless potential of human endeavor. As a young man, he'd even believed he could bend other men to his will by staring into their eyes. It had so unnerved the neighbors that his father made him promise to stop.

Now, Day would subject himself to the ultimate test—to create a new city from wilderness. And if he succeeded, that would be proof that God's grace had fallen upon him.

So when he inspected land, Day did more than calculate the number of citrus trees the soil and rainfall would support. He tried to see the future. He tried to envision how people would live and what they could make of themselves. His comment about the beach, where a man could "have a thirty-mile trot," was certainly an oracle of things to come. And when he looked through the dense copse of trees lining the riverbank, he saw what he was looking for: a beautiful city with wide, tree-lined thoroughfares and ample lots for gardens and children's games. A good place to live and raise a family through good times and bad, where people would grow strong and healthy in the sunshine and clean air. Remote enough from the world that the Godly virtues of thrift and hard work would be essentials. He saw, in other words, the perfect antithesis to the smokestack cities he had left behind. So he brought in surveyors to plat out his dream, exactly as he envisioned it, then headed back to Ohio to recruit pioneers.

Seventeen settlers arrived with him that winter. More would follow. Very likely, they were surprised to reach the wilderness and find a town that would be recognizable to many of today's inhabitants. Nothing more permanent than a latrine had been built, but surveyors' chains had already marked out roads and home lots just as

What's in a Name?

Volusia County is a historical oddity. Today, nearly a century and a half after it was established, no one knows where the name Volusia comes from or what it means. In all likelihood, it takes its name from the settlement of Volusia Landing on the St. Johns River, but no record has ever been found that explains how Volusia Landing acquired its name, or why the Florida legislature gave that name to the entire county in 1854. Writers and historians have offered three possibilities over the years: (1) It was named for a French or Belgian trader named Veluche. But no reference is ever made to such a man in any land and title records. (2) The word is Indian, perhaps that of a village or chief. Many Florida names do come from Indians, but the "V" sound is not known to exist in any Native American language. (3) It is a classical reference, perhaps to Volusias, a tutor mentioned by the Roman Emperor Marcus Aurelias in his book Meditations, a standard on ethics and morality in a classical education. If so, it is a very obscure reference to a mere historical footnote. The suggestion is purely speculative. And it is possible that the real answer will never be discovered.

Sea turtle eggs were a rare and much-prized delicacy for pioneers. Both the eggs and the turtles remained popular until they were added to the Endangered Species List.

they exist now in the historic sections of downtown. Beach Street and Ridgewood Avenue followed what had once been Indian trails, then, later, plantation roads, but they had been widened with future growth in mind. Most of the other streets in the old downtown section had been planned by Day, and the home lots platted.

The women in that first group of settlers boarded with the Bostroms while the men sawed lumber and built a roomy, two-story hotel called Colony House, where settlers could lodge until their homes were built. The hotel was complete, but roofing shingles had not arrived on time, so the settlers topped it with palmetto fronds. After that, it was called the Palmetto House, later, the Palmetto Hotel, and remained in operation until it burned to the ground in 1923.

As it happened though, Day's dream was to take root without him. Two years after founding the colony, his manufacturing business in Mansfield, Ohio, began to falter and he had to return there to give it his personal attention. His colony had never made him any money—he'd sold lots for as little as $25—and without revenue from his Mansfield operations, he defaulted on the $8,000 mortgage. Two townsmen, Charles Jackson and W.P. Burr, assumed the mortgage and finally paid it off. Though Day would visit off and on through the years, he would never play an active part in the community's affairs.

But the town survived, and later, as a city, thrived, just as Day had believed it would. Today, when the most modern-thinking city planners sit down to draw up a new community, they look for many of the same qualities Day laid out for Daytona. And if you take a leisurely walk through the city's historic district and the neighborhoods that surround it, you still get a feel for just how Day saw the future. When the time came to name their settlement, the settlers kicked around a few ideas—Daytown, Daytonia. Finally, they settled on Daytona, forever linking the city with the man who first dreamed of it.

Of course, most people who came to Florida in those days were not as concerned with divine grace as Day. It was "King Orange" that brought them, and it was the orange grove that was now bringing the Halifax area back from the ruin of the plantation era. During the Civil War, there had been just five families in the entire eastern portion of Volusia County, three of them survivors of a second colony at New Smyrna that had been wiped out by Seminoles. Just two families lived on the Halifax.

The western county grew much quicker. The St. Johns River connected it to the port at Jacksonville and steamships regularly ran up and down the river. More than a thousand people lived in Enterprise (then the county seat), Deland and Volusia Landing.

With no reliable transportation, Daytona's growth was slow, but its emergence as a successful town was unmistakable. A year after its founding, William Jackson was running a general store on Beach Street. The next year saw the first school, followed by a sawmill, a public hall for meetings and church services, and a stagecoach line to St. Augustine running three times a week. Finally, in 1876, the twenty-five adult men eligible to vote did so, and Daytona became an incorporated town by a vote

Above: As a youth, Mathias Day practiced mind control. He believed he could influence people by staring long and hard into their eyes. All he accomplished was convincing people that he was a very strange young man.

Below: The Palmetto House was the home of many settlers arriving in Daytona Beach until they could build their own homes. This is a later picture, after a second story was added. The Palmetto House operated as a hotel until it burned.

of 23 to 2. The most pressing urban issue of the day was wild hogs causing a nuisance in the streets. A hog control ordinance quickly passed.

The deprivations of frontier life remained, of course. At Palmetto House there were regular card games, and the grand prize was flea powder. The Spanish had not named the area "Mosquito" for nothing. Not only were the tiny, biting insects a pest, they carried malaria and other fevers, and before the town had two schools, it would have two cemeteries. In those days, people did not know that mosquitoes carried diseases, so they did not look to the open water tanks and surface wells where mosquitoes bred as sources of danger. Fortunately, artesian wells were discovered and the fever epidemics eased.

Depredation did not outweigh opportunity in the minds of most Halifax pioneers. Hard work and a little luck were all you really needed to get ahead. Pioneering wasn't brain surgery, after all. It was back-breaking labor, and it paid off. If you survived the fevers, and the hard freezes that came along every three or four years didn't destroy your orchards, then you saw your standard of living increase year by year. And the increase was measurable. A new house . . . new land . . . new orchard . . . new mule . . . new cow. And the intangibles were important, too. Pride in a community you helped build. The respect of your neighbors.

City of Vera Cruz

The days when Daytona could bill itself "The World's Most Famous Beach" were still many years away, but the city did make international news just ten years after Mathias Day settled it. In 1880, a hurricane sank the steamship City of Vera Cruz, en route from New York to Mexico. The hurricane hit midday on August 28. The ship was overloaded with cargo, namely hundreds of barrels of lard, which the crew began pitching over the deck to lighten the craft. But the engine room flooded sometime after midnight and the ship foundered about 6 a.m.

Passengers and crew who were able to stay above water in the storm clung to the ship as long as they could, an ordeal made harder by all the lard that now floated freely on the surface. Some children were lashed to the deck, but the force of the pounding surf flayed the skin from their bones. In the end, only eight crewmen and three passengers out of eighty-two reached shore alive. All of the women and children drowned.

Dead bodies, their clothes torn away by the violent sea, washed ashore and many were buried in a mass grave in the dunes between Daytona and Ormond. Much of the lard washed ashore as well, and as macabre as it may seem to modern readers, the settlers greedily gathered it and used it for cooking. Such were the realities of frontier life—a year's supply of lard simply couldn't be ignored. There were uglier realities as well. For weeks following the wreck, a citizens vigilante group patrolled the beach to prevent settlers from stealing the rings and other jewelry off the bloated corpses as they washed ashore.

New Britain

That brings us back to Andrew Bostrom and his brother, Charley, because no one along the Halifax was more respected by their neighbors. The Bostroms were decent boat builders. They were better orange growers. But they really left their mark as innkeepers. And for so many people who came to the Halifax, their home was the first stop.

In the days before the stage line opened, many people reached the Halifax by walking the twenty-five miles from Matanzas Inlet. Most of that walk was shear murder, through soft sand on a steep slope that made you limp and left you with a backache. Mercifully, toward the end of a long day, you reached a stretch of hard sand with a rake so subtle it was nearly even. Better still, you soon saw footprints in the sand, a sure sign of civilization. Then, at long last, you came to a weathered post with "Bostrom's" painted on it, and a sandy trail cleared through the brush and dunes. Another half mile along that trail and you reached the sweet-scented paradise the Bostrom brothers had built on the eastern shore of the Halifax River.

When you arrived, you were greeted with the same fine hospitality that had greeted Mathias Day. The Bostroms served a fine meal, offered a comfortable bed, and in the morning took you hunting or sailing or sightseeing, depending on your pleasure. And most remarkably, you didn't have to pay if you weren't able. One pioneer, Chauncy Bacon, arrived with a wife and child and fifty cents in his pocket. The wife and child boarded with the Bostroms for several months, free of charge, until Bacon had built a home. Better neighbors are hard to imagine.

Three years after Day had settled Daytona, a trio of men from New Britain, Connecticut—Daniel Wilson, George Millard and Lucious Summers—made their

Right: The Day family of Mansfield, Ohio. Mathias Day is standing at right.

way down the beach and found themselves at the Bostrom home. They worked for the Corbin Lock Company, and their employer, Philip Corbin, had sent them to Florida to find land for a new colony. The Bostroms squired them around miles and miles of Halifax country, but finally, the men decided there was no better place than where they had started. So they bought 810 acres of the Henry Yonge plantation, across the river from the Bostroms. The Yonge grant was then owned by Rudolphus Swift, a timberman whose once-thriving family business was dwindling now that fewer ships were made of wood. Altogether, twelve New Britain families would divide the Yonge grant and settle it.

The next year, when the men returned to clear the land, they met young Loomis Day, son of Mathias. Loomis was suffering from a persistent upper respiratory infection and wintering in Florida on his doctor's advice. Loomis had no real work to do and spent a good deal of time sailing on the river. The New Britain men offered him some work helping them clear their land and Loomis, otherwise rather bored, accepted. One day, Wilson asked Loomis for a favor. Wilson needed to sail his boat to Port Orange, where his wife and two children were waiting for him along with some new settlers. The party had come by steamship down the St. Johns to Enterprise, then rented a wagon and driver to take them to Port Orange. Wilson was afraid his boat wasn't big enough for all of them, so he asked Loomis to join him with his own boat.

Loomis was always helpful enough, but he was a young man with very little direction in his life. The New Britain men had asked him to throw in with them, but he'd remained noncommittal. That is, until he met the Wilson daughter, young Miss Emily, a pretty, fresh-faced girl with wavy blonde hair and porcelain skin who rode in Loomis's boat back to the New Britain colony. Her presence meant *"the twelve miles up to Bostrom's were not a bit tedious for me,"* he would write in his diary, *"and I did not care how long it took to negotiate them."* Emily would become the colony's deputy postmistress, and it was never a mystery why young men would stop by every day to check for mail that rarely arrived more than once a week.

The young Day, though, had suddenly found a purpose in life, and began spending all his time at the New Britain colony. He helped build a bunkhouse where the men could work and sleep while the women stayed with the Bostroms. When one of the men decided against moving his family to Florida, Day bought up his share of riverfront and orange grove. In the spring, when most of the New Britain men returned to Connecticut to work another season at the Corbin Lock Company, Day stayed on with the Wilson family to tend the groves, carrying buckets of water by hand to each tree on the 182-acre grove.

The Wilsons took over a cabin abandoned by Swift and his lumberjacks. The cabin, like the rough men who had built it, was infested with fleas. So Day and the Wilsons spent a day hauling salt water from the river and keeping the walls and floors saturated all day. That took care of the fleas, though Loomis would write in his diary that he *"didn't*

Plantation Number Nine

There is no better example of a Halifax pioneer than Chauncy Bacon, who took possession of his 172-acre orchard in 1876 with little more than an ax, a hoe, fifty cents in his pocket and a top hat on his head. Bacon, a Civil War veteran and struggling architect from Connecticut, chanced everything he had on a trip to Florida and a piece of beachside property. The day he arrived he hung his top hat on a tree, cleared enough brush for a campfire, dug a well, used the ax to notch shelves into a live oak tree, and built a lean-to of poles and palmetto leaves. As the sun set he lit his fire, then his pipe, stretched out on the ground, and, thinking of a favorite story he'd read years before in Scribner's Magazine, gave his modest plot the audacious name Number Nine Plantation. His incongruous top hat eventually earned him the nickname "Duke of Number Nine" from his neighbors.

The next day he began clearing scrub. It took a year before his fields were ready to plant. His palmetto shelter was replaced by a two-story house atop a Timucuan shell mound. Eventually he would have about 1,500 producing orange trees and a similar number of nursery trees. When he began to grow more than he could ship, his two-story home became a jelly factory under his wife's management. He built the family a new two-story home with mahogany panels and mantels carved with illustrations of Indians. The mahogany was salvaged from the City of Vera Cruz wreck. His jellies and jams became famous and the Number Nine Plantation became a regular tourist destination. Today, his elegant third home still stands, fitting quite nicely into the upper-middle-class subdivision that has grown up around it.

know whether we drowned them or disgusted them." Once the cabin was habitable, he joined the Wilsons as their boarder.

Log cabins were a step up from thatched huts. John Anderson bought the property where he would later build The Ormond Hotel because he found a log cabin there that was ready to move into.

His courtship of Emily Wilson took more than a year. They were married March 2, 1875, in the settlement's first wedding. The colony had grown considerably in that time, but the pioneers still led a frontier life. There was no new material for Emily's wedding gown and no music for the ceremony. There was no church, and nearly no minister. They had to send to New Smyrna for a preacher, and he almost drowned in a storm before getting there. On the way to their honeymoon in Deland, the bride and groom were attacked by an alligator, though only a wagon wheel sustained injury.

Among the things the new colony lacked was a name. Most people called it New Britain, like the city they'd left behind, but that was never official. It also lacked a real identity. Nothing set it apart from all the other orange grove settlements springing up in Florida. For that, the pioneers would have to await the arrival of two men, one of them an old settler with a name and legacy that belonged to the past, the other a new settler with a vision to match the future.

Stephen Crane, author of The Red Badge of Courage, *was on his way to Cuba to cover the Spanish-American War for a New York newspaper when his ship, the* Commodore, *sank 12 miles off the coast of Daytona Beach after striking a sandbar. Crane, like most of the passengers and crew, made it safely to shore, but not before losing his money belt with $700 in gold coins. Crane later wrote a short story,* The Open Boat, *based on the incident.*

Shipwrecks were a source of much-needed raw materials for isolated settlers. The photo above is the Cobb House in Ormond Beach, built from the wreck of the *Nathan Cobb*. The name of the schooner at left is not known.

Freed Men

The first attempt to establish a permanent, postwar settlement on the Halifax was made by African American war veterans and freed slaves. (There were some lumber and turpentine camps but they were seasonal and never attempted to become towns.) The settlement failed, but it did leave behind its name—Port Orange—and a few families who became some of the oldest in the area.

Unfortunately, when it comes to the history of Port Orange, the same problem arises as with much of black history in the region—it is mostly told by white men. In the diaries and letters left behind by plantation owners and white settlers, there will be some mention of a favored house servant here, a runaway slave there, but nothing comprehensive, and few personalities emerge. Nevertheless, they were there, from the introduction of slavery on, and perhaps earlier, with the first migration of Creek Indians who may have brought escaped slaves with them from Georgia.

The Port Orange settlement was the idea of John Hawks, a white abolitionist and physician from New Hampshire who had served as a medical officer with a black regiment during the Civil War. After the war, he helped start the Florida Land and Lumber Company with the intention of settling black war veterans on fifty-acre homesteads. Federal law allowed freed slaves to buy government land at greatly discounted rates in Florida and other Southern states. To Hawks, this looked like a win-win proposition for both himself and the blacks he would help settle. He would have a ready source of labor for his sawmills, and blacks would have steady employment while they cleared and planted their land. Most of the homesteads were just north of Mosquito Inlet (today called Ponce de León Inlet) on either side of the river. Hawks called his settlement Port Orange for the most prosaic of reasons. He'd scanned a registry of post offices and found none anywhere in the United States with the name Port Orange. This, in the days before zip codes, would make it more likely that his mail reached him.

While the settlement's failure by most historical accounts is blamed on sandy soil—the story goes that the freed slaves disliked it and simply moved on—there were other, more prominent reasons, many of them detailed in the research of Dr. Leonard Lempel, a history professor at Bethune-Cookman College. For one, Hawks, though well intentioned, was not the most competent businessman. The lumbermill he ordered was much more sophisticated than he needed, and never was made operational. Worse still, he was one of the few honest white men to involve himself in homesteading. One agent brought 1,000 blacks to settle alongside the Hawks community at Port Orange, but absconded with all the government supplies earmarked for the freedmen. The Port Orange settlers shared their resources with the new arrivals, but it put a disastrous strain on both groups. Later, the treasurer of the Florida Land and Lumber Company made off with the treasury, and a federal Freedman Bureau employee stole rations earmarked for black pioneers. That combination was enough to doom the colony.

Hawks, though still had a significant role to play in the development of the Halifax. After the failure of his lumber business, he became a land agent. In 1870, he was with Andrew Bostrom when they met Mathias Day, and helped persuade him to look at land on the Halifax. He also founded a town called Hawks Point (another solo entry in the post office registry) which later became the city of Edgewater. And his books The East Coast of Florida and The Florida Gazetteer are two of the primary sources for the region's history.

Most of the black families Hawks brought to Florida moved on. A few, totaling less than a hundred people, remained on the Halifax. Most of them moved a little further north, taking the post office and the name Port Orange with them. They settled on property that had been part of the Dun-Lawton plantation, and later was incorporated as the city of Port Orange. A few families remained on their original homesteads, in what is today the town of Ponce Park. And some joined the Daytona colony when it began. Two black men, Thadeus Goodin and John Tolliver, were among the twenty-five men who voted to incorporate Daytona in 1876. It was their road construction company that bid for a series of contracts to finish the plans Mathias Day had laid out for Ridgewood Avenue.

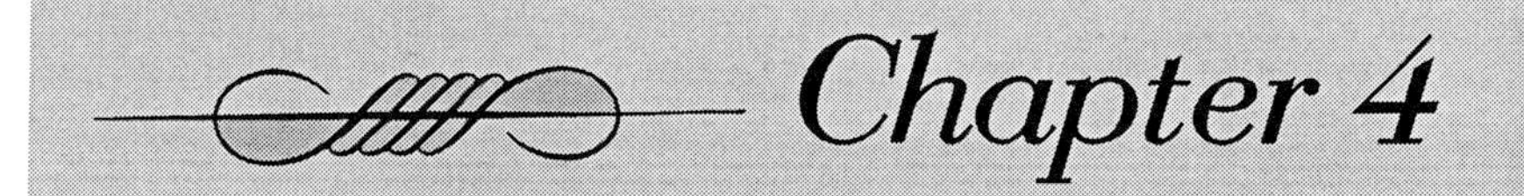

*T*HE *W*AR *Y*EARS

Waiting for a Train

John Anderson was twenty-two years old and had been toiling in the bond and exchange departments of New York City's top banking firms for three years. His prescription for success was simple: "My best *for* the best."

So at first glance, everything would seem in order: A young man with a keen mind and boundless energy, his eyes fixed firmly on the future, employed by the very banking houses that were raising a new nation from the embers of the Civil War. His formal education was not the finest, but he'd done as much with it as any man could. At his public high school, he'd organized a drill team that competed with actual regiments and won a commendation from President Ulysses S. Grant. Following a short course at business college, he'd landed a series of jobs that put him shoulder to shoulder with graduates from Harvard and Yale. Many of them would fall by the side in the great panic of '73, but Anderson held his job. Moved up, in fact.

Left: Steam and sail ruled the Halifax before the railroads came.

The future was bright New York was poised to become the world's financial capital, and Anderson was along for the ride. But something was yawning in his young soul—something that wasn't filled by working ten-hour days, six days a week, inching his way along the endless leviathan of facts, figures and paperwork. Every day he passed newsstands with their penny-dreadful pulp magazines promising romance and adventure on the frontier, where brave men and women were carving out new lives and a new society. These images must have sparked memories of his own happiest times, tramping through the woods near his home in Portland, Maine, a favorite rifle or shotgun resting on his shoulder, the hardy laughter of young men echoing through the trees as they checked their traps and kept an eye peeled for bear. Small wonder, then, that all it took was a letter from his friend and cousin, Sam Dow, to change John Anderson's life forever.

"I have found God's country," Dow wrote. *"The hunting is good and the chances for a young man to show his grit and nerve were never better. Come on!"* The country he was writing about was the New Britain colony on the Halifax River. Anderson, having never set foot in Florida, packed a trunk, left behind his bright career and headed due south to become a pioneer.

One day, soon after Anderson arrived, he and Dow were exploring the beachside, looking for good property to start a grove. As they walked along they heard a strange sound, like women weeping in the woods. They followed the sound and found two women sitting on a high platform. The platform, roughly hammered and swaying beneath their weight, was built fifteen feet above the ground on stilts. The two men called to them, asking if they needed help. Their husbands were on the mainland, the women said, clearing land for an orange grove, and had built the platform for protection from bears. One of the women said a bear had wandered into their

John Anderson left Wall Street to look for adventure and opportunity on the Halifax. He and his partners built the Ormond Hotel, then sold it to railroad tycoon Henry Flagler, making Ormond a favorite winter destination for the wealthy.

Joseph Price, one of "The Boys" in pioneer Ormond. Along with his friend and partner, John Anderson, he built and managed the Ormond Hotel for many years.

bedroom just two nights earlier, and they had been spending their days above ground and out of reach ever since.

To someone like Anderson, long accustomed to roughing it, bears could be a nuisance, but not something to drive you up a tree—or platform, in this case. These people clearly weren't cut out for the life they'd chosen. Their cabin, on the other hand, suited him fine, and the property was just what he and Dow had been looking for. Knowing the prospect of a good deal when he saw it, Anderson asked the women if they might want to sell out. Yes, they said. Most assuredly. Without a doubt. Could he come back when their husbands were home and talk it over with them? He and Dow returned two days later and found all four pioneers ready to throw in the towel. They were in no mood for haggling. A hundred dollars, they asked, just enough to get them home. Anderson and Dow talked it over and made a counteroffer—a hundred and twenty-five, just so they could feel they weren't taking advantage of the hapless quartet.

Anderson couldn't know how important those eighty acres would become. Or maybe he did, as he was always brimming with self-confidence and bright ideas. But his immediate plans were to get to work, grow some oranges and have a little fun. With Dow and another young man, Charlie Fox, they moved in and named their new cabin "Trappers Lodge." They immediately discovered another trio of young bachelors living nearby. Joe Price, Jack Thomas and Elijah Craig, all of Covington, Kentucky, were living in a cabin they called "Hammock House."

All six young men became fast friends, and a large piece of beachside real estate had taken on the virile air of a nineteenth-century bachelor's paradise. There was plenty of time after all the hoeing and planting to hunt and fish and just knock around the woods. Many of the colonists took a paternal interest in "The Boys," as the six young men became known, bringing them garden produce and other amenities. The boys repaid them with lavish parties they called "The Bachelors' Socials." These were no small affairs. The bachelors would roast one deer and smoke another, bake pies, cook vegetables. They had a good recipe for black bear, too. For decorations they mocked the conventions of home life and domestic bliss by hanging shotguns, fishing nets, axes and anti-marriage slogans from the walls. Anderson would take up his fiddle and Price, his flute, and the two of them would lead the townspeople through dozens of square dances.

Over the years, the parties continued, but the six bachelors became five, then four, and so on, as nature took its course. Finally, only Anderson was left, and he would never marry. But he'd formed a strong bond with Price, whose children would always call Anderson "Uncle Jack." Price was trained as a civil engineer, which coupled nicely with Anderson's background in finance, and the two men would work side by side for most of their lives.

Living History

No one really knows why the old man made his way to Trappers Lodge. Surely he knew what he was looking for wouldn't be found so near the beach. It's possible someone in town sent him that way—maybe the Wilsons; their post office would be a likely first stop. Maybe they figured that Anderson would know, if anyone did, where to find the plantation ruins the old man was looking for. After all, Anderson was the county tax assessor now, not for any interest in a political career, but because it gave him an excuse to ride, camp and wander for days in the woods, exploring and mapping.

Anderson could find some interesting things, that was sure. Like an old, deserted causeway built through the swamps along Thompson Creek. It was just a section of road, built up high and lined on either side with palm trees. But it was like finding the lost tribe of Israel, it was so strange, abandoned and alone in thick jungle like that. Where had it started and where had it led? Who'd built it and where had they come from? And what had become of them?

As it turned out, it was part of the King's Road built by the English in the 18th century. In uncovering the road, Anderson had also uncovered a bit of history that these transplanted Yankees had neither heard nor dreamed of. They knew that their own homesteads were on land that had once been part of Southern plantations, but they had little or no idea of the great English plantations that had been there before, or of the French and Spanish who had explored these lands for centuries before that.

Anderson was always finding strange things. Evidence of Seminoles who'd lived and fought here, and evidence of older, unknown people. Mostly they'd just left behind the old, overgrown mounds of oyster shells and broken pottery, but Anderson had found some of their burial mounds—ancient bones wrapped in bundles along with jewelry and weapons and such. Most people just assumed, wrongly, that the Seminoles had evolved from the earlier tribes.

So whatever led the old man to Anderson's door had brought him to the right place, because he was himself a piece of history, a part of the undiscovered country ready to come into the light.

"My name is Ormond," the old man told Anderson. "James Ormond."

It was forty-five years since the Battle of Dun-Lawton and Coacoochee's short-lived victory over the Mosquito Roarers. Ormond had lived an eventful life since then. He'd

Citrus brought people back to the Halifax area after the Civil War. Groves like the one pictured below produced some of the finest oranges and grapefruit in the world. Hard freezes in the 1890's destroyed many of the groves, and the industry was quickly eclipsed by tourism.

Old ruins like the one pictured above were a mystery to many settlers arriving in the 1880's with little knowledge of the area's history.

married a young woman who'd escaped a Seminole raid near her Tallahassee home when she was just a girl. The girl, Elizabeth Chaires, had fled her home just in time, then hid in the woods, covered with a dark cloak, while the Seminoles killed her mother and two younger sisters. James Ormond had heard the story before he ever met Elizabeth. He wrote to her and struck up a correspondence and friendship. He fell in love without ever laying eyes on her. When they finally met, he took her in his arms without saying a word and kissed her. Elizabeth was shocked, then outraged. It was unspeakable conduct toward a lady in the Victorian era. But she fell in love anyway and they married.

Their lives would always be full of fortune, both good and bad. Each had been homeless more than once, and filthy rich in between. As the Civil War opened, Ormond was doing quite well for himself in Atlanta. When Sherman began his siege, Ormond was too old to be drafted, but volunteered to defend the city. Instead, he was sent to Andersonville, the infamous prisoner-of-war camp where 12,000 Union soldiers died of starvation and disease. Ormond was put in charge of the last 3,200 prisoners and charged with taking them to Jacksonville. But there was nothing left in Georgia—nothing but starvation—and Ormond couldn't feed the prisoners, so he turned them loose, gave them safe-passage papers, and told them to make their way to Union lines as best they could.

When the war finally ended, Ormond joined Elizabeth and their children in Canada. She had managed to sneak $1,000 in gold past the Union troops that occupied Atlanta by sewing it into her clothing. The family moved to England and lived there for several years before returning to Atlanta.

Now Ormond was nearing his eightieth birthday. He wanted one more thing in the winter of his life—to see again the home of his youth, Damietta. He wanted to visit his father's grave there, and perhaps lay to rest a few ghosts before giving up his own. So, with his son Robert, he'd made the difficult journey to the Halifax and found himself on John Anderson's front porch.

Anderson didn't know where Damietta was, but he was more than willing to hunt for it. He and Ormond took a liking to one another, the weary old Confederate and the brash young Yankee. Anderson liked nothing in the world better than a good story, and old man Ormond was full of them. He told Anderson all about the Seminoles, and about the slaves who had once cleared all this land and made it right for cotton and cane. He told Anderson about his grandfather, the Scottish ship's captain who'd been killed by a runaway slave. And about his own father, who came to America to escape a debtors' prison in London. And about his mother, who'd gone mad waiting for his father to send for her. Some of these stories he told as they sat around a campfire their first night out. Early the next day they found Damietta, and in a small clearing they came upon the grave and marker of James Ormond II. They cleared away the brush and roots that had covered it for years, and said a short prayer. The elder Ormond knew where he was now, and he led Anderson and Robert to the plantation house his father had built for his poor mad mother. All that was left was a single chimney. Ormond got down on his hands and knees and began clearing away a half century of leaves until he finally held a few shattered pieces of his mother's best blue china in his trembling hands.

James Ormond III's search for his father's grave and the home of his youth gave Halifax pioneers some insight into a history many had never known existed. The city of Ormond beach is named for him.

The Ormonds stayed on in the New Britain colony for a week. They made some good friends, including the Bostroms. And James, who had felt so near the end of his time, would return each winter and stay in the new house the Bostroms had built, a lovely three-story home they called "Bosavare," Swedish for "home place." It must have done him some good, since the old man managed to make it down for another ten winters.

James Ormond, like so many men and women who had walked the banks of the Halifax, had made his contribution to its rich history, but it was a history quickly buried and forgotten as the fertile earth moved time and again with astonishing swiftness to reclaim what humanity had taken for its own. New trees and scrub quickly covered all evidence of previous civilizations—the Timucua, the French, the Spanish, the English and the Seminole, each in their turn, leaving very little for the eye to find. In the process, the history of James Ormond and his mother's blue china had been covered as well.

But Ormond was to make a lasting contribution with his return. When the settlers of the New Britain colony decided to incorporate in 1880, many had assumed the colony's name would be New Britain, just like the city they had left behind. But the colony had grown considerably by the addition of many families from Illinois and Indiana, and some of them objected to the name. Anderson suggested the name Ormond. Charley Bostrom seconded it. One New Britain man offered a pound of sugar to anyone who voted for the name New Britain, but Ormond carried the day. The official minutes of the meeting don't give a reason. Anderson and Bostrom probably just liked the name and wanted to honor their friend.

Mr. Flagler Comes to Town

There was a newspaper published on the Halifax in those days, *The East Coast Gazette.* It was a fine paper if you wanted to know that the whole town of Ormond ate gingerbread after they elected Daniel Wilson mayor. What they really needed was a Wall Street Journal bureau with a couple of experienced business reporters to deliver some penetrating analysis of consumer shifts and industry trends. Maybe one of them could've figured out why Anderson and Price decided to build a seventy-five room, luxury hotel in the middle of nowhere.

Florian Mann (right), published the Halifax Journal *in Daytona, and* The Coast Gazette *in Ormond (below). His Masonic pin is visible on his vest. Freemasons played an important role in the political development of the Halifax area.*

Granted, transportation had improved a bit in the 1880s. First there had been Buck's Stage Line, with stops in Daytona and Ormond. A traveler could go by rail from New York to Jacksonville in about four days. Buck could get you the rest of the way in another three without fail. Sometimes less. But only if the steamships were running on time. Next came the St. Johns and Halifax River Railroad. The workers had no trouble laying the rail through high, sandy pine country, but they had a devil of a time when they reached the swamps north of the Tomoka River. It took a solid year to run the track through there. They dumped one carload of dirt after another into the marshland and just watched it disappear. Finally they solved the problem by laying a road of crisscrossed logs that held the dirt. The railroad arrived in Ormond in November 1886, more than a year late.

Loomis Day later recalled that awe-inspiring moment. Workers were still laying rail ahead of the train as it inched its way toward town. It was pulled by a tiny locomotive that wobbled along on narrow rails just three feet apart. It burned wood instead of coal and that caused it to throw up sparks from the bell-shaped stack. *"It acted as if it had had a couple of drinks on the way over from Palatka,"* he wrote. This, by the way, was not the construction locomotive used to haul material to the workers. It was the flagship engine. The workers had already pitched the construction locomotive into the swamp to get it out of the way. Day made the trip over to Daytona in December to watch the train arrive there. By that time the workers were so frustrated they were just slapping the rails right down on the bare ground without bothering to build a bed.

The new railroad, no matter how comical, was a godsend for most of the settlers. Produce could leave and supplies arrive on regular schedules now. Gone forever were

Buck's Stage Line opened the first overland route between the Halifax and the shipping and train lines of Jacksonville. It was a tenuous connection to the larger world, though. The trip was hard, and passengers sometimes had to get out and push.

the days when citrus rotted because rainstorms made the wagon roads impassable, or steamship delays caused whole towns to exhaust their supply of food staples.

But that doesn't explain why Anderson and Price thought they could make a go of it with a big hotel, especially one on the beachside, which was still wild bear country and only approachable by boat. The new railroad, after all, still didn't connect the Halifax to the wider world, just to the St. Johns River. It was the major cities of the north and midwest that Anderson and Price needed to reach, as well as a new generation of traveler.

Since the Civil War, people had come to Florida for their health, usually on the advice of their doctor. One family to make that trip was the Flaglers of New York. Henry Flagler was partners with John D. Rockefeller in the Standard Oil Company, the richest corporation in the United States. In 1878, he had brought his wife, Mary, to Florida on her doctor's advice. They stayed in Jacksonville, at that time a rather rough port city with few accommodations suitable for one of the world's richest and busiest men. Neither Flagler nor his wife were very happy with their trip, but the sunshine and sea air did their unmistakable work and Mary returned to New York in finer health than she had enjoyed in many years. Mary's doctor wanted her to return the next winter, but Henry refused to leave his business affairs. He urged Mary to go on alone, but she refused to leave without him and became critically ill. Henry made last-minute preparations for both of them to return to Florida, but Mary quickly became too ill to travel and died.

It was a hard lesson for Flagler, but it opened his eyes in other ways. In 1883, he came to Florida with a new Mrs. Flagler on their honeymoon. They stayed in St. Augustine. This time Flagler saw the state as a potential tourist mecca. It was on another visit, in 1885, during a local celebration of Juan Ponce de Leon's discovery

of Florida, that Flagler's ideas took their final form. By this time, the Standard Oil Company was churning along more or less on its own. The management practices that Rockefeller and Flagler had initiated were being carried on by new men. Rockefeller was devoting most of his time to the foundations he'd established, and Flagler, too, was ready for new challenges.

Flagler would later say the Ponce de León festival gave him the idea to build a hotel in the Spanish explorer's honor. More likely he saw the potential revenue of transforming St. Augustine into a Mediterranean theme park. At the time there were fewer traces of Spanish influence to be found. Other than the old fort, the Castillo de San Marcos, the oldest buildings dated back only to the English occupation. Most of the small city had been built since Florida had become an American territory. But Flagler brought in the New York architect Thomas Hastings and instructed him to

build three Spanish-style hotels. In 1888, the Ponce de León, the Alcazar and the Cordova opened. Suddenly St. Augustine—and eventually the rest of Florida—had a Spanish influence that was entirely out of proportion to the actual colonizing by the Spanish. But Flagler had no intention of celebrating a cold, damp climate like Great Britain's. He wanted to bring the sunny Mediterranean within reach, and not merely to invalids and semi-invalids under a doctor's care. He wanted to attract anyone wealthy enough to afford a winter residence. The wealthy, after all, were drawn by more than a simple desire to escape the cold winters. The smokestacks and soot of the industrial north were a health hazard even in the summer months. As Daytona historian Harold Cardwell points out, the annual trip to Florida extended life. *"People arrived with bodies choked by carcinogens and went home well. It was therapeutic, almost a convalescence. They could exercise, visit the springs and splash in the ocean, then dine on fresh seafood, citrus, honey and pickled sand pears, figs and guavas,"* reports Cardwell.

Left: The first passenger train to reach Daytona arrived a year late. Workers were so frustrated and harassed, they began to lay track on the bare ground in the final days. This engine was the flagship of the St. Johns and Halifax River Train Railroad. It would soon make way for the larger Florida East Coast Railway of Henry Flagler.

In today's age of fax machines and cellular phones, it's hard to imagine a wealthy industrialist leaving his empire for three months every year with no more than a telegraph line connecting him to his lieutenants. But the advantages were very real. In the northern cities, the average life expectancy was about forty-five years, a mere ten years higher than it had been in the days of Caesar and Cleopatra. But the robber barons of the era, who could afford to safeguard their health, routinely lived into their eighties and nineties.

That still doesn't explain Anderson's interest in building a hotel, though. If anything, one would think Flagler's plans might have discouraged him. It was a hard trip to the Halifax for rich people, and once there, they still had to worry about bears and alligators. But Anderson's plans took shape anyway, usually just a step behind Flagler's. While Flagler was building the first leg of his grand Florida East Coast Railway, Anderson was encouraging Stephen Van Cullen White, a wealthy Wall Street broker with family in Florida, to pour his money into the rickety St. Johns and Halifax River Railroad. While Flagler was busy laying out a new city in St. Augustine, Anderson was again talking White into spending his money, this time on a narrow wooden bridge to the beachside of the Halifax. And when Flagler opened his three palatial hotels, their accommodations fit for royalty, Anderson was just starting construction of his wood-frame, seventy-five room hotel on property that people had avoided developing for about 5,000 years. At every step of the way, Anderson was not only a step behind Flagler, but his effort appeared pale and dingy by comparison.

But the truth may be that Anderson, the one-time Wall Street banker, and White, the wealthy stockbroker, were making some very shrewd judgments. Unfortunately for the writers of history, people did not take public pride in their shrewdness back

The first train station in Daytona Beach.

then. In interviews, or in their own writings, businessmen held forth with only the noblest of motives. For instance, a Henry Flagler would say he built a hotel because he wanted to honor Ponce de León, *not* because he was the first smart guy on the scene and knew before anyone else that he could make bucketfuls of money doing it. Or, a John Anderson would say that he wanted to spread Ormond's name around the world, *not* that he could see Flagler and his money coming from a long way off.

Anderson, White, and to a lesser extent, Price, must have realized that Flagler and Rockefeller were the most successful monopolists of their age. They did not really believe, as Adam Smith had, that competition made for better industry. Competition merely cut into your bottom line, as far as they were concerned. Most of their business practices are illegal today, as Congress over the years attempted to legislate into existence the rules of capitalism that Smith had theorized as natural laws. The robber-baron method was to eliminate your competitors—buy them out if possible, drive them out if necessary. White and Anderson appear to have gone into the hotel and transportation business with the sole intent of being bought out.

Top right: Excursions on the Tomoka River were a favorite of the winter guests at hotels in Ormond and Daytona. The man seated at far right is holding a pennant from Cornell University.

Bottom right: The very proper lady in the bow of this boat is probably taking aim at an alligator. Alligators posed a threat to early settlers, but when tourists began shooting them for sport, the population quickly dwindled.

The key to that plan would have been the railroad. As near to worthless as the St. Johns and Halifax River Railroad was, White and his partners had proven they could build one on the land they owned. That was important because if Flagler was to extend his railroad south, as he was certain to do, he would rather not repeat the experiences of the St. Johns and Halifax near Tomoka. Better to just buy the railroad that was already there, tear up the cheap track and lay down his own. Which is just what Flagler did. And if someone already has a bridge across the river, even if it's so narrow two wheelbarrows couldn't pass one another, better to buy it, too. It might not serve your needs, but you'll keep the other guy from expanding his

Some Florida cowboys eating their lunch. The word "cracker" may have come from their practice of driving cattle ahead of them by cracking whips.

own business to compete with yours. And if, on the other side of that bridge, someone has built a hotel, then you'd better buy that, too. Even if the builder didn't share your idea of turning Florida into a Mediterranean theme park, and went and built something that looks like it ought to be on Cape Cod, you still don't need the competition. If it's cheaper to buy them out than drive them out, then that's the way you go.

It was on that last point the plan almost hit a snag. We don't know how much Anderson, Price and White, who had again put up the funding, asked for it, but ultimately they got about $120,000. A good sum in those days, but it's reasonable to assume they were shooting for something much higher, probably in the neighborhood of a quarter million or more.

Why didn't they get more? Because Flagler engaged in a classic negotiating tactic—he started to bargain with a third party to get the same thing. In this case, the third party was William Jackson, the most prosperous businessman in Daytona, owner of Jackson's Island, Jackson's General Store and Jackson Hall. It was the island Flagler was interested in. He expressed interest in building his own hotel there, Jackson offered the island to him for nothing, just to draw some of the Flagler fortune to struggling Daytona.

Anderson and Price, meanwhile, could not afford to let their deal slip away. They not only owned the hotel, but the land surrounding it, which was sure to be developed once Flagler improved the property. So they agreed to Flagler's price. They also worked out a plan, though no one can say for sure whose idea it was, that they would stay on as managers. This not only guaranteed them employment, but more important, allowed them to direct the affairs of the hotel in such a way that their other property would increase in value. Once the Ormond deal was closed, Flagler went back to Jackson and added an unreasonable stipulation to the deal for the island. Free wasn't good enough. Flagler also wanted to be tax-exempt for thirty years. Healthy optimism for a man of sixty. Jackson turned him down, and the Hotel Ormond became the newest jewel in Flagler's crown.

In 1922, Helen Sawyer, Anderson's longtime secretary, wrote about him in the *Daytona Daily News* with elegiac reverence.

> *[He and Price] working together, decided that what Ormond needed in order to make it grow was a big hotel, right on the river-front, where they could gather people from all over the United States and who on their return would spread the fame of Ormond abroad. . . .People told them they were crazy. . . .*

That is how Anderson and Price are still remembered and written about today. Visionaries, straight from the movie *Field of Dreams*, who proved the world wrong and elevated themselves to the status of patron saints. Never mind that it was Flagler who had the idea first, and that every step they took seems directed merely at cashing in on the old robber baron's *modus operandi.* After all, Flagler would have built a hotel if they hadn't. But if they were more shrewd than visionary, then celebrate their shrewdness. They nearly played him like a fiddle. Flagler would build his Florida East Coast Railway all the way to Key West, but the Hotel Ormond was the only hotel he would buy rather than build himself. In many regards, it would be his most successful hotel. And no one else along Florida's long coast came close to getting the deal that Anderson and Price made.

Divorce, Florida Style

Henry Flagler, son of an itinerant Presbyterian preacher and the product of a broken home, was shrewd, bold and utterly unscrupulous. He was also a towering figure in Florida history. He created the state's tourism industry, opened South Florida to development and routinely whipped the legislature like a red-headed stepchild. And he did all this after the age of sixty, when he had already helped build the biggest, richest company in the United States—Standard Oil.

Flagler was a grain merchant in Bellvue, Ohio, when he teamed up with John D. Rockefeller and went into the oil business. Standard Oil worked hard at being a monopoly and Flagler was the chief architect of two key components. He invented the trust, in which companies are combined through legal agreements. That practice was outlawed in 1890 by the Sherman Antitrust Act. He also developed a railway monopoly through a series of brilliantly devious contracts that all but forced other oil companies to join the Standard Trust or go out of business. That practice, too, was halted, this time by federal regulation of interstate rail traffic.

But coming to Florida gave him a loophole. Since the Florida East Coast Railway did not cross state lines, it was beyond federal regulation. His plan to extend the railway all the way to Key West was part of a larger scheme to create a new monopoly that could not be broken by federal legislation. Because Key West was the southernmost extension of the United States—just ninety miles from Cuba and three hundred miles closer to the Panama Canal than any other U.S. port—Flagler wanted to make it the major port of entry for all goods from South America and the Caribbean. His monopoly railroad would then make him the sole source of distribution to all points north.

Olds Hall, started by Ransom Olds as a nondenominational retirement home for missionaries and ministers, is an outstanding example of the influence Henry Flagler's hotels had on Florida.

Flagler never realized his dream. He simply ran out of time. He would pour most of his personal fortune into the Key West extension in an effort to see it completed in his lifetime. He did manage to make it to Key West on the first train to complete the cross-ocean journey. That was in 1912, when he was 82 years old and in poor health. He died the next year and the company's directors soon abandoned his most ambitious scheme.

Flagler was a man of great charm, but also ruthless cunning. He had his second wife, Ida Alice, locked away in a sanitarium and had her declared insane. Some

The Ormond Hotel undergoing its first expansion and renovation after Henry Flagler purchased it.

The Ormond as it looked many years later. The old hotel stayed open longer than any of Flagler's other hotels. Its wood-frame structure made it a fire hazard, though, and it was torn down in 1994.

reports said she clearly was delusional, but others said that she was just socially inept, a working-class girl unable to adapt to the upper-crust society that her husband, some thirty years her senior, handled with ease and charm. In other words, she embarrassed him, and it was not unknown in those days for women to be declared insane when their husbands could not control them. By that time Flagler had a new lady, Mary Lily Keenan, but could not divorce his second wife under New York law. So he changed his residence to Florida and strong-armed the legislature into a passing bill—the Flagler Divorce Law—that would dissolve only one marriage—his. Eleven days later he married a third time. His bride was 36, he was 72.

Now whether you view Flagler as corrupt and immoral, or simply ahead of his time on no-fault divorce, there is no question that he brought the first real prosperity many Floridians had ever known. Just ten years after his railroad first passed through the Halifax country, tourism had outgrown agriculture as the area's major industry. There were also plainly human and sympathetic touches to the man. During the Great Freeze of 1895, many North Florida farmers faced starvation. Flagler ordered his employees to distribute food and supplies at no charge to make certain no one was hungry.

Henry Flagler is one of the most important people in Florida's history. He made tourism an industry, built railroads and opened South Florida to development.

*T*HE *G*OLDEN *A*GE

Winters of Contentment

William K. Vanderbilt was awfully good at a number of things. He could captain his own sixty-five-foot yacht, seduce another man's wife or recite from memory all the best wines in all the best cellars of New York City. But the thing he did best was spend his grandfather's fortune. He spent money with a style and daring that actually made people admire him. His grandfather, Cornelius Vanderbilt, or the "Commodore," as he had people call him, built that fortune with steam engines. Steamboats and steam locomotives, the back bearers of the Industrial Revolution. He'd done well enough that grandson Willy never had to worry about his gambling losses, or anything so mundane as work. Oh, Willy had a job of sorts. He was a railroad tycoon, if anyone asked. But the truth was he'd have a hard time finding a locomotive if he began his search from his own private Pullman car.

Left: An early race on Daytona Beach.

No, Vanderbilt preferred to think of himself as a sportsman, and other men who dressed in white pants and straw-boater hats took him quite seriously. He'd won the America's Cup, after all, the world's premier yachting event. Those were the days when a boat from the New York Yacht Club always won. Always. They even had the cup bolted to its showcase. It was Willy's turn to win back in '95. That had been swell. Something the old man never did. But the glory was fading. Besides, his own son was proving to be a better yachtsman and would win the cup three times. Better card player, too. Invented a game he called contract bridge.

Well, old Willy Vanderbilt wasn't going to let the 20th century get too tight a grip on things without making some kind of name for himself. And Ormond Beach was just the place for that. Why, just last year all the papers had buzzed about Alexander Winton when he set a new speed record on the sand. Automobile racing was the thing now. Very modern. The way Vanderbilt saw it, he could blaze a trail with gasoline engines the way the Commodore had with steam engines. Speed. It was all anyone talked about at the club that fall. Who would set a new record at Ormond this year?

Vanderbilt had an answer, and it was under the bonnet of his new, German-built Mercedes-Benz, with its narrow, hard rubber tires and a radiator grill shaped like home plate. He was proud of his car, confident of its abilities. But as he donned his racing cap and goggles the morning of January 27, 1904, positioned himself on the wooden bench behind that big, four-cylinder, 90 horse-power engine and felt the cool ocean mist brushing his cheeks, he had to wonder if this was really the day he would be the fastest man alive. Did driver and machine together have what it took to top Winton's record of 68 mph?

Five miles later, the middle one being the official, or "measured" mile, Vanderbilt had his answer. An unbelievable 92.3 mph. The cheering crowd rushed to surround him. Reporters shouted questions. Someone handed him a bottle of champagne.

William K. Vanderbilt on his 90 horsepower Mercedes. The wealthy playboy set a world record in 1904, covering a mile in 39 seconds.

Photographers wanted his picture. Soon the news would spread around the world. A new, official land speed record. If you wanted to go faster than Vanderbilt, you'd have to fall out of a window.

It was amazing how much things changed with the 20th century. Someone finds oil in Texas, someone else flies a motorized glider at Kitty Hawk, a fellow in Switzerland says that E=MC2, and suddenly you're living in a whole new world. And few places in the world had changed more than the Halifax. The pioneers were still there, but their pioneering was done. Tourism was the leading industry now, especially after a hard freeze in 1894 decimated many citrus groves. Daytona, Ormond and the smaller towns that were springing up around them had learned that their destiny was to be a destination. Henry Flagler's railroad was doing its job, depositing rich people by the carload throughout the winter, then rounding them up for the trip home each spring.

At center stage, ringmaster, camp counselor and arch provocateur, was John Anderson, proving year after year that nobody threw a party like he did. Flagler could steer wealthy guests his way, and Joe Price did a splendid job overseeing various expansions and additions, but it was Anderson who applied the magic touch. It was his off-key irreverence and wit that transformed Ormond—both the town and the hotel—into some Edwardian wonderland of easy grace and pointless endeavor to delight the wintering wealthy.

Above: Alexander Winton in his Bullet. Winton was a bicycle builder who's interest in cars brought him to the sands of Daytona and Ormond. He set a world record in 1903 that was never officially recognized because the speed trials lacked a governing body.

Right: John Anderson, mounted on a horse and carrying a lance for one of The Ormond's "Ring Tournaments" on the beach. It was one of many amusements Anderson planned for his wealthy winter guests.

It took more than trains to bring the ruling class so far from their stately mansions. It took publicity, and Anderson had a knack for that. Among the glittering likes of the Astors and Vanderbilts, he sprinkled in his own guests. They were writers, artists and the occasional newspaperman, all of them thrilled to rub elbows with the silk-and-satin set, and ready to tell the world when they returned home. Anderson even managed to have the oranges and other citrus grown along the Halifax proclaimed "the best in the world" at a fair in New Orleans. It was a dubious claim. The fair actually went broke before it could award him a trophy. No problem. Anderson had one struck himself. Then he sent photographs and press releases to every major newspaper in the country.

Meanwhile, Anderson and Price put Flagler's money to good use. They built a ballroom where ladies and gentlemen in the finest fashions could waltz to the orchestra he kept in residence. Hotel rooms were lit by electrical generators brought down from the Chicago World's Fair. Guests could stretch their legs on the walking paths he cleared, or ride about in wicker wheelchairs pushed by young, black porters—the guests called them "Afromobiles"—sometimes racing up and down the beach. They played golf on imported Bermuda grass at two courses built near the hotel. The latest silent films played in Anderson's theater, accompanied by a pianist. Sometimes the movie stars themselves, were seated in the audience. He sponsored medieval "jousts" with guests dressed as armored knights and courtly ladies, and each year crowned the "Queen of Love and Beauty" at a pageant. He built a ballpark and recruited a professional baseball team to amuse patrons. When the ballplayers weren't on the field, they worked as waiters in the grand dining room.

Above: Contestants in a bathing beauty contest organized by John Anderson.

Below: Surf sailing was a popular activity at the turn of the century.

There was nothing Anderson wouldn't try to keep his guests entertained. So when J. F. Hathaway, who wrote about automobiles for several newspapers and magazines, told him he should sponsor races on the beach, Anderson jumped at the idea. Hathaway had brought one of the first automobiles in Florida to Ormond and had made a name for himself frightening cows in the village. One day, while watching a bicycle race on the beach, he'd noticed how the tires left virtually no imprint on the sand. He thought it would make an excellent course for cars.

The first race was held in 1902. Ransom Olds brought his Pirate, an odd, spidery contraption, all chassis and no body. He rode behind the water-cooled, single-cylinder engine in a sulky, the kind of two-wheeled buggy with stirrups used by riders in harness racing. Alexander Winton drove his Bullet, a high-chassied affair that ran along on four wooden wheels. They competed in speed trials, where each driver made his run separately. The goal was not to see who crossed the finish line first, but who covered the "flying mile" in the least time.

As it happened, the first speed trial on the beach, perhaps in the entire country, ended in a tie. The best time posted by each man was 57 seconds.

The next year, both men were back with improved cars. This time Anderson and Price had filled their hotel with newspaper writers to witness the event. But someone nearly managed to sabotage the whole affair. Members of the Jacksonville Automobile Association objected to the race as a publicity stunt to draw tourists away from that city. Apparently some member of the club was responsible for sending out dozens of telegrams announcing that the event had been canceled. So, many drivers, as well as spectators, stayed away. Nevertheless, the trials went on as scheduled, and this time there was a clear winner. Winton posted a record time of 52.2 seconds on the mile. The news spread around the world from the tiny Ormond telegraph office, where journalists filed their stories. Winton would be feted at Madison Square Garden for his achievement, and his beloved Bullet would end up in the Smithsonian Institute.

Ransom Olds's improved Pirate may have been the loser that day, but it did him no lasting harm. He was to sell 3,750 "Oldsmobiles" that year, making him the early leader in automobile production.

Below: The Ormond Garage, built by Henry Flagler for the 1904 speed trials, was used for many years by professional drivers and automotive designers to repair and test their machines before attempting new records on the beach.

The race was notable for one other reason. Anderson and Price had begun referring to their course as Ormond-Daytona Beach, since it now extended that far. As the course grew longer still, Daytona's name would replace Ormond's on the dateline of most stories, and the fame associated with auto racing would shift forever away from Ormond.

The following year, in 1904, when Vanderbilt made his winning run, there were two more significant additions. This time, Anderson and Price dodged the controversy of the previous year by enlisting the fledgling American Automobile Association to sanction the event, making Vanderbilt's record the first "official" time in auto racing. They also went to Flagler for more money, this time to build a garage big enough to significantly increase the number of competitors. Flagler gave them the money for what became the famous Ormond Garage, the original "Gasoline Alley." But he had his doubts. He didn't really think their racing scheme would ever get off the ground. Flagler firmly believed it was golf that would make the Ormond-Daytona area famous.

In the crowd, watching Vanderbilt's accomplishment that day, was a forty-year-old man almost no one noticed. His name was Henry Ford, and he had brought his own car down from Michigan to race, but had to leave it in the Ormond Garage because he was too broke to fix an axle. He'd just sunk all his savings into a venture—the Ford Motor Company—and so far had not seen a dime of profit. So he watched from the grandstands an event that still very much belonged to wealthy enthusiasts, like Vanderbilt. That would all soon change. The very next year cars routinely ran more than 100 mph and two men, a driver and a mechanic, were killed on the course. By 1905, the speed trials had become an international event. The world's best automobile manufacturers hired professional drivers to test the experimental models. Vanderbilt would be back in 1905, but he finished back in the pack, three seconds off his best time the previous year. Far from dominating the world of auto racing, he was to be merely a footnote.

Mystery S

The year was 1927, and there was more than one reason for excitement the day Major Henry Segrave arrived from Southampton, England, with his three-ton crate and his team of four engineers, six mechanics and a corps contingent of British journalists and newsreel photographers. The biggest reason was in the crate. The first time Segrave rolled his "Mystery S" out of the Ormond Garage, the locals got a look at something the likes of which few people had ever seen. The term "science fiction" had not been coined yet, but it would have been an apt description of Segrave's futuristic midnight blue racer, a product of the British Sunbeam Motorcar Co. It looked like something H. G. Wells would have dreamed up to fly to the moon, or maybe Edgar Rice Burroughs's idea of what would pass for a flying chariot on Barsoom. It was, in fact, simply a car, but one designed to do what no other car had done—reach speeds of 200 mph.

There was another reason for excitement. Segrave, lanky, balding and aristocratic, was about to breathe some new life into the Halifax. Between 1905 and 1920, six land speed records had fallen on Daytona Beach, but for seven years no one had attempted a new mark. The reasons are somewhat nebulous. Certainly, racing had been hurt by the early deaths of the two men who had built Gasoline Alley and made the Halifax area famous. Anderson and Price had both died suddenly in 1911, within a month of one another. The tourism industry chugged along without them, but they were truly irreplaceable. There would never again be such an amazing font of ideas and initiatives in the area.

Also, the Roaring Twenties had ushered in the great Florida land boom, especially in Daytona. Sub-divisions were springing up everywhere, with speculators sometimes buying and selling a single lot of land as often as six times a day. All of Florida was booming, but Daytona was particularly attractive to developers. The beautifully planned city that Mathias Day had laid out had only been enhanced through the years. Artesian wells fed numerous fountains, and attractions such as the public Burgoyne Casino on Beach Street and numerous reasonably priced hotels and guest houses made the city appealing to budget-minded families. While Ormond remained an enclave for the rich, Daytona was bringing the dream of sunny winters within reach of the growing middle class.

Paradoxically, as faster race cars shortened the distance between Daytona and Ormond, the economic realities were moving them farther apart. Ormond remained stable, Northern in character, affluent and progressively Republican. Daytona was growing, becoming increasingly

Ransom Olds, left, seated behind the wheel—er, make that stick—of an early model Oldsmobile.

Southern, blue collar and Democratic. And because of a large population of African-Americans who had settled there to work on the railroads, it was becoming a target for Ku Klux Klan activity and influence. Such barbarity was unheard of just a few short miles north in Ormond. The cities were no longer in sync, and in many ways they were ready to turn their backs on one another. The decline of speed racing was partly a result of that.

There was one other reason people had to be thankful for Segrave's arrival, though it could hardly have occurred to anyone at the time. The Great Depression was just around the corner, and Daytona in particular would suffer from it. In a few short years, cash would become as rare as it had been to the first pioneers, and many people would be living off the land as surely as the Timucuans had, fishing, shucking oysters and planting vegetable gardens to keep from starving. The land boom would end and tourism would be all but dead. For a small city that had learned to live on the money it made between January and mid-April each year, the Great Depression would nearly be a death knell. The town would grow so quiet that gangsters like John Dillinger and Ma Barker and her crew began spending their winters there. "The World's Most Famous Beach" would become a good place to lie low. But Segrave and his comrades, and the renewed interest in racing they brought with them, at least gave Daytona some semblance of a season to look forward to.

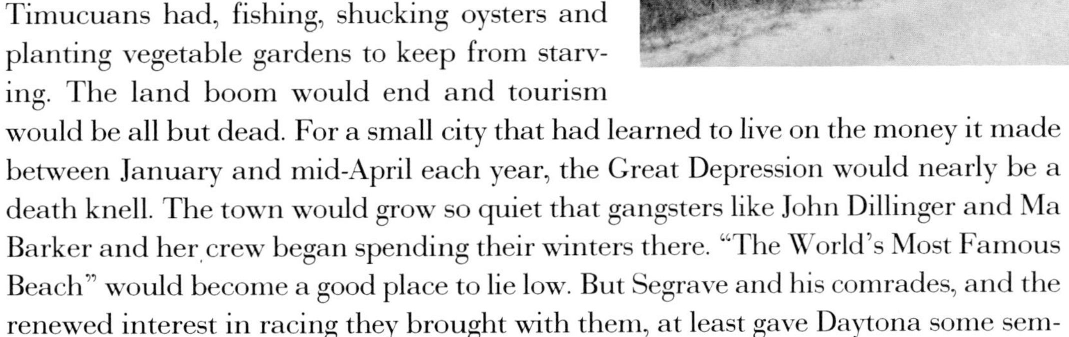

Above: J. F. Hathaway first noticed that bicycle tires left no deep impressions in the hard sand near his favorite winter getaway, the Ormond Hotel. He suggested to John Anderson that the beach would make a good track for automobiles, and the rest is history.

But all of that was still in the future when Segrave first arrived, delivering his massive crate to the Ormond Garage on a giant flatbed truck. For two weeks, Segrave kept a low profile, adhering to a Spartan training regime that had him up before dawn for calisthenics and a look at the beach. There was no smoking and no drinking, nothing at all to dull the five senses. His senses and reflexes were all he would have when the time came to make 200 mph across the beach. At that speed, wind resistance would buffet his car like a major hurricane. The slightest skid could send him crashing into the surf, or worse, tumbling into the grandstands. Each day he checked the beach, and each day it failed to satisfy him, until finally a thunderstorm left the sand packed as hard as concrete. He decided that this would be it and gave the word. Someone ran with the news to the fire station on Beach Street, and someone there cranked up the siren. Everyone in town could hear it, and everyone knew what it meant. Soon, thousands of people lined the beach, waiting for a glimpse of the Mystery S.

Below: Headquarters of the East Florida Auto Association, which ran the speed trials at Daytona and Ormond. The "39" sign is to commemorate the 39-second mile that William K. Vanderbilt drove to establish the first recognized land speed record.

The nine-mile course Segrave had selected began at Ponce Inlet and stretched north. He would have four miles to reach top speed, then the measured mile, then four miles to slow and stop. Then he would turn his car around and repeat it. Segrave had once promised his wife he would never die in a car accident, but just as the car was ready, he betrayed his anxiety and asked for a cigarette. Then

The hard sand of Daytona Beach made it as easy to land airplanes there as it was to drive cars. The first airport was on the beach. Pictured here is Ruth Ann Law, a pioneering aviatrix and the first woman to fly a plane in Florida.

for fifteen minutes he chain smoked, taking a cigarette from anyone who offered one. Finally with everything ready, he donned a crash helmet. He was the first driver in America to wear one. There was concern that in his open cockpit, the smallest insect or seashell—anything at all—might leave a fatal impact on his skull.

To the spectators, the Mystery S, some fifteen feet long, driven by twin aircraft engines, appeared to go by in a flash, first to the north, then, on the return leg to the south. Within minutes, the news flashed around the world. Segrave had covered his mile at an average speed of 203.79 mph. After thanking everyone in Daytona Beach, he returned to England for a gala celebration and a knighthood. Sir Henry Segrave had started a new era of motor speed. And in Daytona Beach, things were happening again.

Lockhart Gambles

The next year, 1928, brought Segrave back to Daytona, but he was not alone. His exploits of the previous year had generated renewed interest on both sides of the Atlantic. Captain Malcolm Campbell was another English driver, and the first to try his luck on the sand that year. His was a new face to Daytona, but not to Segrave.

The two military men had been testing themselves against one another in cars and on speedboats for half a dozen years before coming to Daytona. Campbell's pride had been deeply wounded when Segrave crashed the 200 mph barrier. But good soldier that he was, there was nothing to do but come to Daytona and attempt to set the mark a little higher, which he did in workmanlike fashion, driving his hand-built Bluebird II at 206.96 mph across the measured mile. Then he packed his car and returned to England, with an air of that's that.

But it wasn't. It was, in fact, nothing but a low-key beginning, because next up was the boy wonder, Frank Lockhart. An American, Lockhart was a proven crowd pleaser. He was short and slight with reddish hair, which gave him an air of Opie Taylor innocence. Two years earlier, he'd won the Indianapolis 500 as a rookie. Not just a rookie, but a last-minute replacement for a veteran driver. And he'd won it in the rain. Already he was a racing legend, the kind of overnight success that America falls in love with.

But there was another side to Lockhart. A desperation born out of tough luck. He had grown up dirt poor in southern California, abandoned by his father. He finished high school barely able to read or write. He probably suffered from dyslexia or some other undiagnosed learning disorder. People who knew him recognized early on that Lockhart had a true genius for engineering, but that his lack of literacy and inability to further his education left him without good job prospects. He could have settled for working in a garage or on a production line, but Lockhart was driven by ideas that were years ahead of their time.

The car he brought to Daytona, for instance, his Black Hawk, was less than half the size of the other beach behemoths. He had increased engine efficiency and developed theories of aerodynamics that clearly pointed the way to the future. But the only way he could build the car was to pay for it himself, and the only way he could prove his ideas was to drive it himself. But if he could win at Daytona Beach, Lockhart was sure he could get the backing for a project that was nearest and dearest to his heart. Less than a year after Lindbergh had crossed the Atlantic in his cramped, single-engine Spirit of Saint Louis, Lockhart was ready to build a four-engine airliner that could make the trip routine. But first he needed a victory at Daytona.

Rain had fallen off and on the morning of his trial, but Lockhart thought that might turn to his advantage. The slightly softened sand might give his tires better traction, and Lockhart needed every advantage he could get. His best time in practice runs had only been 180 mph. As the Black Hawk made its northward run, the crowd could hear the difference in Lockhart's engine design. Instead of the thunderous roaring of Segrave's and Campbell's cars, Lockhart approached with a high-pitched whining.

Everything was going fine. On the last stretch before the measured mile, Lockhart had reached 200 mph and he was still accelerating. Then, suddenly, a

storm cloud that had been hovering over the ocean sent a brief but heavy shower of rain across the beach. Lockhart was driving blind. First the car began to swerve, Lockhart corrected it, but next the car lurched and began flipping end over end until it landed in the surf. A wave crashed over the tiny car, but when it had passed, Lockhart raised his hand to signal he was all right. The crowd expelled its collective breath in a roar of relief. But then another wave crashed. And another. Lockhart wasn't getting out of the car. Someone cried, "He'll drown!" And spectators began racing for the beach.

Lockhart's legs were pinned inside the car. One man stood beside him, holding his head above the water, then covering his nose and mouth as each new wave crashed over them. Someone else got hold of a tow rope and tied it to the car, then dozens of spectators pulled the car from the surf.

Above: For weeks, Henry Segrave kept his Sunbeam Mystery "S" under wraps.

Below: Major Henry Segrave, hoisted aloft by well-wishers after breaking the 200-mph mark on the beach. Segrave would be knighted for his achievement, which opened a new era of speed trials in Daytona Beach.

Lockhart was dazed and frightened. He'd never learned to swim and was deathly afraid of water. He was twenty-five years old and against all odds would live to see his twenty-sixth birthday in two weeks. Remarkably, he suffered no injuries worse than a few sprains and bruises and his sturdy little car was not severely damaged either. So, scraping together his last few dollars, Lockhart began to repair the car. He wanted one more run before the trials were over.

But Lockhart's task was made harder by the next competitor. Ray Keech was a professional driver from Philadelphia. Another Philadelphian, industrialist James White, wanted an American to hold the speed record, so he hired Keech to drive his massive Triplex, a blunt, six-wheeled behemoth that ran on three twelve-cylinder Liberty Aircraft engines. The car was all power with no finesse, and Keech frankly hated it. It shook violently and was hard to control. But if anyone could tame the beast, it was Keech, one of the toughest and most resourceful drivers in the country.

It took everything Keech had just to bring in the four-ton Triplex. Midway through his run a hose disconnected and scalded him with boiling engine coolant. By the end of the race he was nearly unconscious from pain and from breathing exhaust fumes. He'd had enough of the car, and vowed never to drive the Triplex again. But he'd also made short work of Campbell's record, delivering a new land speed record of 207.55 mph, about half a mile faster than Campbell's run.

That set the stage for Lockhart's return in late April. He'd sunk all the money he had into repairing his Black Hawk. Shortly before this final run, his seamstress mother had wired him. She was in serious financial trouble and asked him for $10. He didn't have the $10. He was flat broke. All he could do was send her words of

Malcolm Campbell, a wealthy broker for Lloyds of London, was an expert at assessing risk. He became the only man to drive 200 mph on the sands of Daytona and not die in a speed-related accident.

Malcolm Campbell behind the wheel of his Bluebird III in 1931. He would set seven new land speed records at Daytona Beach.

encouragement. "Ma, I have the world by the horns. You'll never have to push a needle again."

His three warm-up runs were nearly perfect. His tires had collected bits of seashell along the way, and someone warned him he needed to change them. But there weren't any more tires, so Lockhart began his run anyway. Spectators would later say they saw a puff of white coming from his right rear tire as it blew. The Black Hawk swerved, lurched and began to roll and tumble down the beach, tearing craters in the sand with each impact. Lockhart was flung from the car and his lifeless body landed in a heap near the spot where his wife was standing. There was no point in checking for a pulse. The face that had once beamed boyish self-confidence had already taken on the gray clay mask of death, and the shrieks and howls of his young wife rose above the groans of thousands of spectators.

Deadly Triplex

As tragic as Lockhart's death had been, his was not the worst accident on the beach. That was to come the following year, 1929.

Segrave was also back in 1929 with a new car that set a tidy new record of 231.44, almost 24 mph faster than Keech's run in the Triplex the year before. Keech, for his part, was sticking to his guns and refused to come to Daytona if it meant driving the Triplex again. Almost to the end, owner Jim White held out hope that Keech would relent, but when the time came, White was forced to find a new driver

Ray Keech (left), the professional race driver who drove the superpowered Triplex faster than 200 mph on the beach. He had the good sense not to try it a second time, avoiding the Triplex wreckage (below).

or drive it himself. He began scratching around for a driver.

The man he found was Lee Bible, owner of a Daytona Beach garage who had worked as a mechanic on the Triplex the previous year. There's no reason to doubt that Bible knew cars inside and out, or that he was a skilled driver. But he was not a skilled race driver, and the decision to put him behind the wheel of the biggest, most powerful car ever built was totally lacking in responsibility.

Bible was entering the fifth mile of his second warm-up run, traveling faster than 200 mph, when the car swerved off the course and headed toward the dunes. It struck a Pathé newsreel photographer, Charles Traub, with gruesome effect. The lower half of Traub's body was torn to pieces. His upper body flew a thousand feet through the air. The Triplex crashed into the dunes, barely missing the grandstands, then plowed through about 200 feet of sand. Bible's body was thrown from the car into the dunes. Spectators began combing the dunes looking for him. The first to see him found him sitting upright, eyes open, as if he'd miraculously survived with no crippling injury. He hadn't, though. That was just the way he landed, and he toppled over dead before anyone could reach him.

The remainder of the speed trials were canceled that year. Campbell's run would have to wait for another year. But by 1930, tragedy had struck twice more, though not at Daytona Beach. Segrave, who had once promised his wife he would never die in an automobile, died in a speedboat, the Miss England II, on an English lake, just after setting a new speed record on water. And Keech, the tough Philadelphia driver with sense enough not to ride the Triplex a second time, died in a fiery crash in Altoona, Pennsylvania. Of the five men who had driven faster than 200 mph, four of them were now dead—Lockhart, Segrave, Bible and Keech.

That left Campbell, a wealthy underwriter for Lloyd's of London committed to risks that no insurer would ever indemnify. Like Segrave he would be knighted by George VI for setting a new record in an English-made car. He called it Bluebird. He called nearly everything Bluebird, all his cars and boats, after the Bluebird of Happiness in Maeterlinck's play. In England, he was a well-respected businessman, decorated for heroism in the Great War. In Daytona Beach, he became both neighbor and patron saint. Sir Malcolm Campbell made Daytona Beach his home in the winter months, punctuating his stay with a new land speed record five times in seven years. There would be no serious challengers to him in Daytona, but Campbell kept risking his neck year in and year out. He had been denied the honor of breaking the 200

Frank Lockhart, the brilliant but illiterate engineer who became a crowd favorite at Daytona, behind the wheel of his Stutz Black Hawk.

The Black Hawk's wreckage.

The Bluebird racing to a new record at Daytona Beach.

mph barrier, so he had set his sights on being the first man to drive 300 miles an hour.

His fastest time in Daytona was 276.82, set on March 7, 1935. The weather had been bad that morning and few people expected him to run, so the turnout was light. For Campbell, it was just another day at the office, but what no one knew was that it was the last speed trial to be run in Daytona. Campbell decided the beach just wasn't the right surface for speeds that high, so the next year he moved his operation to the Bonneville Salt Flats of Utah, where he successfully punched his hole through the 300 mph barrier. Daytona Beach could still claim to be "The World's Most Famous Beach." But for all the world, it looked as if her greatest exploits were behind her.

John D. Rockefeller

John D. Rockefeller was the world's first billionaire and the wealthiest man alive when he moved to Ormond in 1918. He had been Henry Flagler's partner in the Standard Oil Company and would rent an entire floor at Flagler's Ormond Hotel before buying a house across the street, the Casements, which still stands today.

Rockefeller wanted to live to the age of 100. There is a story that he charged his lieutenants with finding the most healthful spot on Earth for him to grow old, and they brought him back the name Ormond. That story probably did as much for tourism as the speed trials did, regardless of its truth. It's just as likely that Rockefeller simply asked his friend Flagler to recommend one of his hotels.

Rockefeller lived an unassuming life in Ormond. He was a widower by this time and confined his social engagements to church and a small Christmas party each year. But he was hardly reclusive, asking people to be called "Neighbor John." He went to the beach to watch the speed trials and played nine holes of golf every day until 1932, when his infirmities grew too great. It was his habit to hand out shiny dimes to children and to anyone who pleased him. The caddie at left is getting a new dime, and so did Sir Malcolm Campbell, who carried the dime with him for luck when he hurled down the beach in his car Bluebird.

Humorist Will Rogers was one of Rockefeller's many famous guests, and when the old oilman won a golf game once, Rogers quipped: "I'm glad to see you win, Mr. Rockefeller. The last time you lost, the price of gasoline went up."

Rockefeller died in 1937, less than three years shy of his 100th birthday.

Chapter 6

Recession and Renaissance

Struggles

J. Saxton Lloyd, the Beach Street car dealer and longtime player in Florida politics, used to tell a story about Mary McLeod Bethune, founder and president of Bethune-Cookman College, that illustrates the times beautifully. One day, Bethune asked Lloyd if he could meet her at her home. Over the years, Lloyd had become an increasingly important benefactor of her school, but Bethune was reluctant to be seen at his Beach Street showroom. Word had gotten around that Lloyd was considering a run for governor. Bethune greeted him at the door, sat him down in her office, and in her round, sonorous voice told him that if he chose to run, she could deliver to him every black vote in Florida. She also promised him the active support of the President of the United States.

Left: Mary McLeod Bethune on the steps of the college she founded, Bethune-Cookman College.

Below: Mary McLeod Bethune learned the art of politics from two of the greatest practitioners of their day, Franklin and Eleanor Roosevelt. The Roosevelts, as early as 1927, fixed on Bethune as a potential ally in their quest for the White House.

Lloyd was flabbergasted. He knew, of course, that Bethune had held various Washington jobs over the years, but they were not cabinet-level posts. Most people assumed that she was a token Negro. But here she was giving him the word of the President of the United States. This woman. A Negro woman. A large, plain Negro woman. Lloyd's surprise was perfectly understandable. This was the heyday of segregation after all. Not only could blacks not register at the ritzy beachside hotels, but a black man was risking his neck if he got caught on the beachside at all after sundown. Lloyd had known Bethune for years. But in all that time he had never imagined the power and influence she could wield.

There was in Bethune, just as there was in her mentor, Franklin Roosevelt, more than a touch of the mandarin. She could reveal herself slowly, in stages, to whom she wanted and in precisely the manner of her choosing. To many, she was a motherly figure, benign and deeply spiritual, who served hot chocolate to her guests and preached simple virtues. To her students, she could be the towering intellect, often the first person to open their young eyes to what it truly meant to be black in America—and she preferred the word "black," a jarring, clattering word in an age when most people were learning to say "Negro" instead of "colored." To many a politician, Franklin Roosevelt included, she was a fellow pol, an operator, shrewd and skilled, with a constituency that was hers to deal. But like a mandarin, she did not wield her power like a cudgel. She became the source of other people's power, and in turn saw a greater share flow back to her.

It is often assumed that Bethune reached the national stage because of her friendship with Eleanor Roosevelt, but that simply isn't true. She had already been appointed to two child welfare conferences during the Coolidge and Hoover administrations. And although her friendship with Eleanor Roosevelt was indeed sincere and profound, what first brought her to the attention of the Roosevelts was her leadership of the National Association of Colored Women's Clubs, with its lobbying office in the nation's capital and its

J. Saxton Lloyd. Anti-Catholic prejudice made him decide not to run for governor.

300,000 members nationwide—or as the Roosevelts preferred to think of them, 300,000 votes. It was a simple fact of life in the first half of the 20th century that for an African American to have any influence, he or she had to bring something to the table. For Bethune, that something was votes.

Under the Roosevelts' tutelage, she learned to play the game even more adroitly. Throughout her public career, Bethune was always organizing and attending conferences. The "why" and "what" of each conference was not as important to her as the "who." Who was in attendance, and how could they be added to her network of political influence. Perhaps the high point of her career were two national conferences on Negro issues she convened in the 1930s. These conferences are not well remembered today because their reports on civil rights, voting rights, integration, education, and other topics were all buried by Southern committee chairmen in the U.S. Senate. But those reports became a blueprint for action over the next thirty years, from anti-lynching laws and armed forces desegregation in the Truman administration, to the omnibus Votings Rights and Civil Rights Acts of the Johnson administration. One reason for the gradual success of those ideas—aside from their inherent rightness—is that a whole generation of black leaders emerged from those conferences from every walk of life—education, labor, civil service, entertainment and others—with a newly coalesced point of view about what needed to be accomplished.

What's more, Bethune had extended her own political network into nearly every black community in America. It made her one of the most powerful players in the political arena and secured her spot on FDR's Negro Cabinet. Calling it a cabinet was simply a way to gloss over the more naked political deal making underway. The black vote was an essential element of the Democratic coalition Roosevelt formed, and it remains so today.

An interesting footnote: Dr. Joseph Taylor, a historian at Bethune-Cookman College and a noted authority on Bethune's national conferences, would many years later attempt to track down and interview the surviving attendees who had emerged as national and regional leaders from those conferences. It turns out that some never actually attended. Bethune had simply added their names to the roles to give her reports more authority. It did. Both friend and foe of Civil Rights saw a united front extending to every corner of the country emerge from those conferences. That impression enhanced Bethune's own influence, and that greater influence helped her and others actually forge that united front when the time came. Deceptive? Yes, but the kind of maneuver that would have made FDR smile in admiration.

As it turned out, Lloyd never ran for governor. He was a prominent Roman Catholic and decided that anti-Catholic bias in the South was just too great. (He still hadn't changed his mind nearly twenty years later when he met with Jack Kennedy at the Princess Issena Hotel. He told the young senator that America wasn't ready for an Irish-Catholic president. Kennedy decided to run anyway.)

Two Worlds

Bethune will be best remembered for her role as a national leader in the civil rights struggle. She was the highest ranking black in the Roosevelt administration, a pivotal figure in integrating the armed forces and Eleanor Roosevelt's partner in founding the United Nations. She is doubtless the greatest national figure to rise from the Halifax region. But her impact on local politics is sometimes overlooked. She and a handful of others helped steer Daytona Beach and the surrounding communities away from a period when fear and corruption ruled the county. And she helped deliver Daytona Beach into a period when it would be known as a model city of the New South.

Along the way, Bethune had some interesting allies. Some were as deeply committed to good government and civil rights as she was. Others weren't. One was a crooked mayor who circled city hall with armed police to keep the National Guard from running him out of office. Another was a grand dragon in the Ku Klux Klan.

One night in early November 1920, Bethune was working late in her office at the Daytona Normal and Industrial Institute, the school that would later become Bethune-Cookman College. The night had become alarmingly dark. Bethune looked out the window and saw that all the streetlights on Second Avenue had gone out. She'd been expecting something like this. Soon, from the direction of Beach Street, she heard a cacophony of car horns and horse hooves. Then came a procession of people masked in white sheets; at their head was a burning cross.

This was not the first time the Ku Klux Klan had made its presence felt. For several years Bethune had spearheaded voter registration in Daytona's three black neighborhoods and the Klan's intimidation had never been far removed. The year

Today, the Mary McLeod Bethune Foundation is housed in the building that was her home during her most prominent years as a civil rights activist.

African-Americans had lived in Daytona since its beginnings, but their numbers swelled when railroad construction began. Workers from citrus groves in the state's interior, displaced by hard freezes, flocked to the east coast, where low-paying railroad jobs were the only work to be found.

1919 had seen passage of the Nineteenth Amendment, giving women the right to vote. Mostly due to Bethune's efforts, Daytona's voter rolls were beginning to swell with the names of black women. The Klan was worried that its slate of candidates might go down in defeat. So maybe a little cross burning would keep these new voters away from the polls.

At the time Bethune's school was mostly for girls, many of whom boarded on the premises. The sight terrified some of the students, dredging up images of the worst violence perpetrated against blacks since slavery. They began to scream. But Bethune was ready. If the Klan had enough clout to get streetlights turned off by the city power company, fine. She ordered the lights in the campus building put out, too, and all the outdoor floodlights turned on. Suddenly, it was the Klan that was standing in a pool of light, being watched by its own unseen enemies who were concealed by the dark. Then from the darkened buildings, her students began to sing spirituals. Timidly at first, then with increasing verve as they saw how paralyzed the almighty KKK had become. The Klansmen, in fact, appeared unnerved. Eventually they began to scatter into the night.

It would be an exaggeration to say that Bethune's actions broke the back of Daytona's KKK that night, but it was a turning point. A reform government was elected to the city commission the next day. The Klan controlled just two of five votes. More importantly, their failure to intimidate a forty-five-year-old Negro woman and a handful of young girls meant they had already passed their high-water mark. In the past, the Klan had rivaled the county's political machine for control, but thereafter would have to seek accommodation with the bosses.

The Leader

Bethune was the daughter of freed slaves from South Carolina, the fifteenth of seventeen children. Most of her brothers and sisters had been born into slavery, so after the war her parents, Samuel and Patsy McLeod, reassembled their family from the various farms and plantations where their children had been sold. Otherwise, little had changed from the days of slavery. The family's five-acre plot could never yield enough to support them, so both Samuel and Patsy continued to work for the whites who had once owned them. The first real sign of opportunity was the opening of a Presbyterian mission school for black children in their hometown of Maysfield. Only one of the family's children could be spared for schooling, and Samuel and Patsy chose Mary.

Bethune made the most of her chance, going on to college under full scholarship, then heading to Chicago for missionary training, again under scholarship. Perhaps the greatest disappointment of her life was her rejection, because of her race, for a missionary post in Africa. But a missionary was what she was, both by training and temperament, and so she found herself returning to the South as a teacher in a series of mission schools.

By 1904 she was ready to start her own school. She was teaching in Palatka at the time and decided to set off for Daytona Beach, where many black workers who built

Henry Flagler's railroad had settled. By this time she was married to Albertus Bethune, a fellow teacher who would later desert her when her career began to eclipse his own. The couple had one child, Albertus, Jr.

What she found in Daytona were two distinct black communities. One was fairly prosperous, its members working, and sometimes even living, side by side with their white neighbors. Their children were schooled from kindergarten on and they supported two churches. To the degree these black residents were segregated from whites, it was by culture and economics, not law. And despite state election laws designed to keep blacks away from the polls, one black man, Joseph Brook Hankerson, had been elected to the city commission, and another, Joseph Coombs, missed election by a single vote.

But the other black community in Daytona, largely composed of the railroad gangs and their families, lived in the worst kind of poverty—well below what many slaves had known. Most had been citrus workers in the state's interiors before the disastrous freezes of the late 1890s. They had come to Daytona because the railroads provided the only work available, and they were exploited horribly. They lived in lean-tos and dilapidated camp houses. Their children grew up ignorant and unprepared for any kind of work that didn't require brute muscle—something their malnutrition hardly prepared them for.

Two views of the poverty that drew Mary McLeod Bethune to Daytona. Many of the camp workers lived in conditions worse than they had known as slaves. Many of the children born in these camps had never even seen a book, much less learned to read.

That these two black communities should stand apart from one another is understandable, if unfortunate. Until the railroad was built, about one in four Daytona residents had been black, and with so many Northerners (many of whom, like Mathias Day, had been adamant abolitionists), the city provided a tolerant climate for racial coexistence. But by 1900 the city was nearly half black, and in a few years would become predominantly black. That created a more volatile mix, especially a generation after the Civil War, when abolitionist ardor had cooled. The older, more established black families saw the new arrivals as a threat to their own security and tried to distance themselves a bit.

It didn't work, of course. Not long after Bethune arrived, signs began to go up everywhere, dividing Daytona into "white" and "colored." Blacks living along Ridgewood Avenue and in other predominantly white areas began to sell their homes under pressure. The Ku Klux Klan, which had faded with the end of Reconstruction, began to reconstitute itself, and a city like Daytona became an obvious target for its activities. They began to segregate the races by violence. Hotels in the towns

Eleanor Roosevelt came to Daytona Beach twice as a guest of Mary McLeod Bethune. The visits helped raise Bethune's national profile.

of Seabreeze and Daytona Beach, small villages that had not yet been incorporated into the larger city, were torched if they admitted blacks. Soon after, blacks would not even be allowed to swim in the ocean.

When Bethune first arrived, it was the railroad workers who most needed her help. The story has often been told of how she began her school with nothing but $1.50 and some old orange crates to use for desks and chairs. The only property she could afford was in a city dump. The sheer desperation of Bethune's mission is often overlooked. The children she took in not only did not know how to read or write, some had never seen a book. They did not know the basics of hygiene and sanitation. Bethune's educational philosophy, directly influenced by the teachings of Booker T. Washington, was well suited to girls who would have little choice but to work as maids and cooks. Washington himself expressed this attitude when he wrote of the "positive dignity in working with the hands when that labor is fortified by a developed brain and a consecrated heart." Following Washington's lead, Bethune's school had two general departments: the academic curriculum from grade school through high school, including religious instruction; and the industrial curriculum, where the girls learned sewing, washing and other marketable skills.

Bethune sustained the school for years by baking sweet potato pies and trooping her young charges to one exclusive hotel after another to sing Negro spirituals for the wealthy winter guests. The first time John D. Rockefeller met Bethune and her students, he offered his standard reward for people who pleased him, a shiny new dime, which went straight into the school treasury. Later, after Bethune had had a chance to work on him, Rockefeller made far more generous donations. She also forged life-long alliances with James Gamble of Proctor & Gamble, who had a winter home in Port Orange, and Thomas White, president of the White Sewing Machine Company, who wintered in Daytona Beach.

There was some initial resistance to Bethune's mission, and much of it came from the established black community, which still wished to see the railroad camps simply fold up and go away. But with the encroachment of legalized segregation and its inherent assault on human dignity, Bethune's mission soon claimed all of black Daytona. Even the oldest and most established black families in Daytona were to feel the effects of isolation.

Howard Thurman, who grew up to be a respected theologian and Wesleyan scholar, was a young boy growing up in Daytona Beach in those days. Years later he described the social structure of the community.

> *[Blacks] formed a closely knit community surrounded by a white world. Daytona Beach and Seabreeze were exclusive tourist areas. I could work in Seabreeze and Daytona Beach, but I was not allowed to spend time there, nor could I be seen there after dark without being threatened. These areas were absolutely off limits after dark. The white community in Daytona itself was "downtown," and no place for loitering. Our freedom of movement was carefully circumscribed, a fact so accepted it was taken for granted. Thus white and black worlds were separated by a wall of quiet hostility and overt suspicion.*

Under this pressure, the distinction between black communities began to crumble, and Bethune soon found herself the political and spiritual leader of most of Daytona is blacks. Thurman wrote:

> *Very often she would come to our church and she would talk of her dreams for Negro youth. . . . Sometimes we attended her Sunday afternoon temperance meetings. The most memorable aspect of those Sunday afternoons was the lack of segregation in the seating arrangements. Many tourists attended, sitting wherever there were empty seats. There was no special section for white people.*

Already Bethune was becoming an early and formidable champion of desegregation. It began with programs held at her own school—whether the speaker was Booker T. Washington or Thomas R. Marshall, the Vice President of the United States, attendance was desegregated. Later she would take the struggle to the beaches and hotels. What is so remarkable about this, a fact that may be lost on people too young to remember the civil rights era, is that Bethune's campaign was making progress even before World War I—several decades before the nation as a whole began to make significant gains in the 1950s and 1960s.

But Mary Bethune's work in the political arena was just beginning.

Machines and Robes

Fred Booth was the kind of newsman you don't come across anymore. He came to Daytona in 1921, at a time when reporters still worked the streets, not their telephones. When one of them got a good story, it was because somebody spilled

the goods, not because the government revealed it in an audit or grand jury report available to the entire public.

There were some advantages to Booth's style of reporting. He had to know his sources better than reporters do today. Had a better sense of when they were lying and whether they knew what they were talking about in the first place. There were some real disadvantages, too. All the important things government did were decided behind closed doors. And if you went to some public official and asked to see his records, you'd probably get laughed at. "Boy, what do you mean *public* records? These are *my* records." So a lot of stories just never got printed.

The Boardwalk, (top left), was one Depression-era WPA project in Daytona Beach. The Bandshell, (bottom left), was another.

But given the limitations of his day, Booth did an awfully good job. He was respected by his colleagues and he made politicians nervous, and that's all any real reporter asks for. He was a small, fiery man, intense and quick to anger, but didn't hold a grudge. He hated sitting behind his desk unless he was ready to write, and spent most of his days walking the streets, making the rounds among his hundreds of sources. He never bothered to own a car. And it didn't hurt that he knew how to drink, either.

Sometime around his retirement in the 1950s, Booth sat down and began to type a short memoir. It included some stories that never made it to press. One of the most interesting is his description of the rivalry between the Ku Klux Klan and the Democratic machine bosses, known as "the Ring." Most old-timers in Daytona remember the Klan and the Ring as allies, but that came later. Booth begins his narration in 1921, less than a year after the Klan marched on Bethune's school for girls. This failure to intimidate the local black leader had indeed begun to shift power away from the Klan. Booth portrays Daytona as a wide open town in the 1920s, as lawless and corrupt as any town in fiction. He wrote:

> *When I arrived the three municipalities [Daytona, Daytona Beach and Seabreeze] were still buzzing about what nearly happened to the wire tappers. Also about a murder.*
>
> *Every winter in those years the so-called wire tappers (con men who got sucker dough by claiming to get race results by tapped wires) kept shop here. Late that spring their house on S. Peninsula was riddled one night by hundreds of rifle bullets. Nobody hit; they had got tipped and were gone.*
>
> *About that same time a young punk, Grady Hams, was called to his front door at night and riddled with bullets. The KKK got the blame for both jobs. The KKK was the chief political opponent of the political rulers of the city and county—very convenient for the rulers, these crimes. KKK members I knew claimed they had to go underground to fight the bosses to avoid reprisals. (The above crimes were never prosecuted.)*

In those days the local political boss was Police Commissioner Jim Titus. Titus reported to the Ring boss, Bert Fish, an attorney in DeLand. Fish ran a corrupt regime. One of his schemes involved the three bridges that crossed the Halifax at Daytona. The bridges had been built by a private company and operated for years as toll bridges. The contract called for them to revert to the county after the franchise lapsed. But the private company's attorney was Fish, so even after the franchise lapsed, the company continued to operate them and citizens kept paying unnecessary tolls.

Ed Armstrong, a corrupt Daytona Beach mayor, was an unintentional ally of the civil rights movement. To swing elections, he registered unprecedented numbers of black voters, just so he could buy those votes with a few dollars.

The Klan, according to Booth's account, managed to get control of Daytona's government in 1922 with a majority of the five-member city commission. But they blew it by staging a big "bring-your-hood" rally on Beach Street that ended in gunplay. A majority of voters were disgusted and voted them out of office, bringing the Fish Ring back to power.

The choice between the Ring and the Klan wasn't a choice between good guys and bad guys. It was a choice between corruption and danger. The Ring had a corrupting influence over the banks, the courts, most of the large companies in the county and the civil services. The Klan's main appeal was to blue-collar whites, who often felt victimized by the Ring's control. And neither side had any use for the city's majority Negro population, which both sides wanted to keep away from the voting polls, unless their votes were bought and paid for.

Then some very interesting things began to happen. First, in early in 1927, Bethune was invited to a luncheon at the home of New York's governor, Franklin Roosevelt. The affair was hosted by his wife, Eleanor, to honor the heads of some two hundred women's clubs. Already the Roosevelt's were beginning to forge the alliances that would lead them to the White House in 1932. The scene was typical of many in Bethune's life. She was there as president of the National Association of Colored Women and the only black present. There was a good deal of tittering and anxiety when the women were called to the dining room. There was a bit of jockeying for chairs because no one wanted to be seated next to "the Negro." FDR's mother, Sara, quickly sensed the confusion and took Bethune by the arm and led her to a seat next to the hostess, Eleanor. By the end of the afternoon, the two Mrs. Roosevelts, who could barely tolerate one another, were both fast friends of Bethune. More importantly, Bethune had made a political alliance that was to provide a boon to the entire Halifax area, particularly to its black citizens, for many years to come.

Also in 1927, Ed Armstrong , a Ring-backed politician, was elected mayor of the recently consolidated city of Daytona Beach. In 1925, Daytona and the two beachside communities, Seabreeze and Daytona Beach, had voted to consolidate following failed efforts to create an even bigger city that would have included Ormond Beach, Holly Hill and Port Orange. The consolidation had been backed by the Ring, but in the first election the Klan managed to win enough seats on the city commission to deny the Ring a majority, according to Booth's insider account. Booth also believed the first mayor of the consolidated city had been a Klansman, though he didn't have it on the man's own authority the way he did so many others. But that government lasted just two years. The land boom was dwindling to a halt by 1927, and that, along with anger from many local businesses who had had their Ring graft cut off, was enough to get Armstrong, a wholesale grocer, elected.

Armstrong stood for reelection in 1929, the year of the great stock market crash and beginning of the Great Depression. It's hard to imagine just how thoroughly devastating the Depression's effects were on the Halifax area. First the banks failed.

The Merchants Bank, the Volusia County Trust and others all went under, taking their depositors' assets with them. In the days before the federal government began to insure bank deposits, this meant that nearly every working family in the Daytona Beach area had its entire savings wiped out. Ring men, sometimes selling their bank stock just days before the closures, became the bank liquidators. Depositors were paid less than 2 percent of their assets.

The next thing to die was tourism. The smaller guest houses along Ridgewood Avenue and Atlantic Boulevard were the first to close their doors, but the larger hotels began to feel the pinch in no time. An economy that had learned to get along on three and a half months of business each year was now faced with no months of business. Tourism was all but dead and buried. On the heels of the Depression would come World War II, with strict gas rationing that made it impossible for most people to even reach Daytona Beach. The era of the wealthy Northern industrialist wintering on the Halifax was over. Those seasonal guests were too busy jumping out of windows when the Depression started. For several years Daytona Beach was so deserted that it became a favored hiding place for gangsters. John Dillinger and Ma Barker came to the area to lie low for awhile. So did Franklin Roosevelt's brother, Edward, who moved there under an assumed name after he married a Bowery prostitute and shamed his family.

Daytona Beach and some of the surrounding communities might have died off altogether if not for the help of some prominent area families. When the banks closed, these prosperous families personally advanced money to the penniless depositors ruined by the bank closures. Their only security was a lien on the same amount of deposits, which were now all but worthless. Hundreds of working families stayed off the breadlines and in their own homes because of that generosity.

Meanwhile, Mayor Armstrong also found himself in a desperate situation. He was facing reelection and the Ring could no longer supply him with graft money. So he came up with some other ideas. First, he made a clean break with Fish and all the other Ring politicians. Then he began to extort money from local merchants. If a merchant didn't contribute to his campaign fund, Armstrong blacklisted him and fired any city employee who shopped there.

When Governor Dave Sholtz tried to remove Armstrong from office, the renegade mayor had his wife appointed to replace him. When Sholtz sent in the National Guard to have her removed, Armstrong ordered armed police to ring City Hall, and hold off the guardsmen.

Next he started to buy votes, and that's where Bethune reenters the picture. Now, the cheapest votes to be had were black votes. White politicians used to joke about rounding up the black vote with a few dollars and a half-pint of whiskey. There was nothing new about buying black votes. Election-law loopholes had been used for years by white employers to register their black employees so they could swing elections with the extra votes. But Armstrong needed black votes on an unprecedented scale, and he was willing to pay whatever he could extort from local merchants to buy them.

Here's where Armstrong's and Bethune's interests coincided because in order to buy black votes, you have to register them first, and that was what Bethune had been trying to do all along. In the 1929 election, black voter registration doubled. By the time Armstrong died in 1937, more than half of the black adults in Daytona Beach were registered. Starting in 1932, Bethune began to deliver the black vote in Daytona and throughout Florida for Franklin Roosevelt.

And both phases of the Roosevelt administration—the Depression-era New Deal and the wartime production era of World War II—sent dividends back to Daytona Beach. Bethune took a job with the National Youth Administration, part of the fabled Works Progress Administration, and WPA projects began to spring up all along the Halifax. The Boardwalk (or Broadwalk as it is officially named) and the Bandshell were WPA projects. So is the downtown Post Office, the Holly Hill city hall, the Armory and several other surviving projects throughout the eastern county.

Bethune no doubt lobbied for those projects, which were the greatest financial windfall the area would enjoy during the Depression, and she had some help from an unlikely team in Congress—Joseph "Little Joe" Hendricks and Senator Claude Pepper. Hendricks was Daytona Beach's congressman in those years and he was also a grand dragon in the Ku Klux Klan. But he found himself a silent partner with Bethune and a public ally of the senator dubbed "Red" Pepper for his left-leaning politics, when it came to bringing WPA projects to the area.

Then, during World War II, Bethune took a job with the War Department, advising the army on recruitment of women officers for the Women's Army Corps. Again, although she never took public credit, Daytona Beach saw a windfall. A training center for WACs opened in Daytona Beach and some 14,000 young uniformed ladies were stationed there between 1942 and 1944. Hotels and guest houses that had been shuttered for years suddenly had paying customers again, because there was no barracks space to house so many women. Daytona Beach also got a taste of the future as well. With another navy pilot school training 4,000 pilots in nearby Ormond Beach, the war years must have looked like one, long "Spring Break" to much of the city.

In all of this, Bethune stayed behind the scenes, always exercising her power like a mandarin, to such a degree that most Daytonians were hardly aware of her or her accomplishments. But it was only the beginning of her legacy, one that would continue to grow long after her death in 1955.

Armstrong managed to stay in office almost continuously thanks to the black vote, but it only gave him the time he needed to build the most notorious reputation

The arrival of the Women's Army Corps in Daytona Beach during World War II opened many of the guest homes and hotels that had been unoccupied since the start of the Depression.

in the history of Daytona Beach politics. The most lurid moment of his administration came in 1936 in a showdown with Florida Governor Dave Sholtz, himself a Daytona Beach politician with Ring ties.

Armstrong had overspent the city budget, giving Sholtz the legal right, under charter, to oust him and the entire city commission and appoint their replacements. But Armstrong got word of the deal before it came down and pulled a fast one. He resigned as mayor and had the commission appoint his wife, Irene, to succeed him. Sholtz was outraged. He ousted the entire commission and replaced them with his own men, then he sent the National Guard to city hall to back up his order. Once again, though, Armstrong was one step ahead of him. First he had all the city records loaded onto city garbage trucks and carried into hiding. Then he had armed city police circle city hall for a showdown with the National Guard. For a time you had the legitimate city commission locked outside, while the renegade grocer, Armstrong, barricaded himself inside with his outlawed commission and his mayor-in-name-only wife.

The showdown ended in a draw. The police weren't willing to face a serious threat from the armed forces and departed, but without the city records, there was

Above: Former Florida Governor Dave Sholtz, a Daytona Beach politician.

Below: Desegregation of Peabody Auditorium in 1948 helped foster Daytona Beach's image as a racially progressive city.

very little the Sholtz-appointed commission could accomplish. That threw the whole matter into the courts. The Florida Supreme Court sided with Armstrong, saying Sholtz had overstepped his authority and that the transfer of power to Irene Armstrong had been legal. But Armstrong died shortly after without ever really regaining control of the government.

Bethune continued her campaign for desegregation at home and across the country. She also saw her tiny school for girls grow into an accredited four-year college after merging it with the Cookman Institute in Jacksonville. In 1948, she and other local black leaders desegregated Peabody Auditorium after a long struggle with the city commission. After that victory, blacks began to challenge the segregation of other public facilities.

Back in the 1920s, Bethune had helped develop a beach for blacks after they were banned from the main beach areas. But in the early 1950s, she began a successful fight to have the entire shoreline of Daytona Beach desegregated. She also succeeded in desegregating the city bus system, both in seating and hiring practices in 1955, a full year before the U.S. Supreme Court banned segregated city buses following the Rosa Parks incident in Alabama.

Bethune had retired as president of Bethune-Cookman College in 1942. A bad heart and other health problems had made it impossible for her to both run the school and pursue her civil rights agenda as she had for so many years. After Franklin Roosevelt's death, Eleanor gave Bethune FDR's silver-headed cane, the one he used for balance whenever he was forced to lock the braces on his crippled legs and stand upright for photographers or to make public speeches. The cane was perfectly suited to Bethune's six-foot frame, and she used it for the last ten years of her life.

It was in the last year of her life, 1955, that Bethune saw so many things she had worked for come to fruition. That was the year she helped desegregate the beaches and buses. It also was the year she helped form the Interracial Advisory Committee, a group of twelve whites and twelve blacks who advised the city on racial issues. In the early 1960s, this committee would play a role, along with the local NAACP and Bethune-Cookman students, in desegregating local lunch counters, parks, the Halifax Hospital, the city golf course, seating at the baseball park, the police department and county grand juries.

Daytona Beach came to be known as a racially progressive city in the 1960s, something backed up by academic studies and judicial reviews. This reputation grew from the ingenuity and sincerity with which both whites and blacks responded to racial problems.

Doctor, Mayor, Woman

Irene Armstrong was not the first woman mayor of Daytona. That distinction belonged to Dr. Mary Josie Rogers, known to most people as Dr. Josie, and also the first female doctor in Daytona. In fact, the whole Armstrong affair left such a bad taste in people's mouths that for years Dr. Josie was referred to as the only woman to be mayor of Daytona.

Rogers was born just four months after Daytona incorporated in 1876. Her father, David Rogers, opened Main Street on the beachside, the first street to cross the peninsula, and built the first of a succession of bridges that crossed the river at the site of the current Main Street Bridge. (These facts can be a little confusing since he called both the street and the bridge Seabreeze, after a resort town in New Jersey. The street and bridge that have those names today got them when the Post Office moved there. The street Rogers built became Main Street when the town of Daytona Beach started.)

Above: Bethune-Cookman College, Daytona Beach's first four-year institution of higher learning.

Politics was nothing but a brief interlude in Dr. Josie's fifty-year medical practice. She won election to the city commission in 1920, the first election after women won the right to vote. She was on the slate of progressive candidates supported by Mary McLeod Bethune and opposed by the Ku Klux Klan when they marched on her school. The mayor was George Marks, who left near the end of his two-year term to become superintendent of schools. As Dr. Josie would tell the story years later, the four men on the commission couldn't decide among themselves who should be mayor, so they compromised and settled on the lone woman serving with them. She served out the remainder of Marks's term, but did not run for reelection to the commission.

For the rest of her life, that brief spell of public service would usually overshadow her medical practice and her many other civic contributions, such as her early support of Bethune's school. And because she was born the same year as the city, whenever Daytona Beach reached a milestone birthday (which, in the years before its centennial, was about every five years), someone would decide to celebrate its first woman mayor as well.

Dr. Josie treated the attention with good humor, and always enjoyed a party. But she rarely spoke of politics or the turbulent years she served. She never mentioned the shoot-outs and rum-running, or how the Klan seized control of the government at the end of her term. She preferred to tell people how she made her house calls on a bicycle because her horse was too spirited to hitch to her buggy. But as the years went on and people kept asking the same stupid questions, she could grow a little cantankerous. When she was in her nineties and was asked for the umpteenth time whether people liked having a woman doctor, she snapped: "I don't remember asking them. They just came. And the ones who didn't I didn't much care about." She died in 1975 at age 98.

Below: Dr. Mary Josie Rogers became mayor of Daytona Beach in 1920, just a few months after women won the right to vote with ratification of the Nineteenth Amendment. She was also the first female doctor in Daytona.

Chapter 7

*P*resent and *F*uture

Castles in the Sand

Try as you might, you really can't separate the history of Daytona Beach from the history of tourism in Daytona Beach. The first settlers along the Halifax River had hardly moved out of their palmetto-thatched huts and into proper homes before lodgers arrived. Even when the Halifax area was remote and isolated, accessible only by a series of boat trips or a 30-mile walk, people still came for the fishing, the hunting and the vibrant natural beauty that Ernst D'Erlach and Mathias Day had written of, separated from one another by 300 years.

History, though, is not a continuous thread. The wealthy guests in hotels like the Clarendon, or the Ridgewood, or the Princess Issena, wintering away the final decades of low taxes and idle riches, would hardly understand the concept of a family vacation—working people, wage earners, who carry their own luggage, taking a week or two to fly to Florida, in the summer of all things, to crowd along the beach or wait in the perpetual lines of Disney World.

Times change. And one way to approach history is through the way times change. As it happens, the history of Daytona Beach can be divided into three eras, each represented by a man who exemplified his times and his city.

Left: Two pelicans get a surprise as a dolphin breaks the surface of the Halifax River. The natural beauty of the region was what first brought tourists.

Below: Two views of tourism. In the 19th century, tourism meant wealthy Northerners spending the entire winter season in residence. The group (top photo) has found a nest of turtle eggs, considered a delicacy at the time, before their popularity put local varieties of sea turtles on the Endangered Species List. A modern family (bottom photo) typifies today's tourist industry—middle-class families spending a week, a weekend, even an afternoon at the beach during summers and holidays.

C. G. Burgoyne

There is an irresistible air of mystery about Charles Grover Burgoyne. He is something like the Ozymandeus of Shelley's poem—nothing of his mighty work remains, just his name on a shattered pedestal in Pinewood Cemetery. In a very real sense, though, he built Daytona as a monument to his own philanthropy, then ruled it from a castle on Beach Street.

By his own account, C. G. Burgoyne was the embodiment of the Horatio Alger myth. Born in 1847 in the town of Fairmont in what would become the state of West Virginia, Burgoyne joined the Union Army as a boy and distinguished himself in the Civil War, tunneling out of a Confederate prison in Richmond. After the war he went to work as a printer, publishing a two-page newspaper for several years, then sought his destiny in New York City, where he arrived with just five cents in his pocket. There, his story goes, he founded the C. G. Burgoyne Printing Company, and developed a revolutionary printing process that made him wealthy. He used to brag that this printing process of his could take a 600-page book from manuscript to bound volume in less than 24 hours, a remarkable feat in those days of movable type.

Another story was that his wealth derived from his invention of the ticket roll, which came into nearly universal usage

Above: Charles Grover Burgoyne in his office at Burgoyne Castle, sometime after 1910.

and is still used today at fairs and carnivals. In any case, after 20 years he left New York a wealthy man, and moved to Daytona Beach.

The mystery surrounding Charles Grover Burgoyne begins with his name, which wasn't Charles Grover at all. He was born Ezra Burgoyne but started calling himself Charles Grover when he moved to New York. There's also some mystery about how he came by all his money. You can scour the various histories of printing and he is not credited with inventing anything. Not the Linotype, not the Monotype, not the ticket roll. Nor is he credited with any advances in hot type technology. That doesn't mean his story isn't true, just that it cannot be verified. Neither can the more scurrilous stories that he made his fortune running gambling rackets and, when things got too hot in New York, introduced the rackets to Daytona Beach. People liked to tell stories about Burgoyne almost as much as he liked to tell them about himself.

He and Mrs. Burgoyne apparently came to Daytona Beach as winter tourists several times before moving there permanently. That was in 1896. He built a home on the beach, accessible only by boat. Here the mystery gets a little deeper, because the Mrs. Burgoyne he brought with him wasn't the same Mrs. Burgoyne he'd had before. His new lady was a dark, young beauty with a low-born accent named Mary MacCauley, and there were some who swore she'd been the personal maid of the previous Mrs. Burgoyne. But Burgoyne soon made it known she'd been a proofreader at his New York company, if that was anyone's business.

A year was about all the seclusion they needed. In 1897, they entered the life and affairs of Daytona in a big way.

Burgoyne had himself elected mayor that year. No mean feat, even for a man with most of the money in town. Daytona was very cliquish in those days. North Beach Street and South Beach Street were very nearly two different towns, each with its own newspaper and social clubs, even its own bridge to the peninsula. An outsider arriving and instantly being elected mayor was unusual, to say the least. But these were hard times—citrus groves were failing and many men were looking for work, and Burgoyne quickly became the leading employer in town. No doubt eliciting a tremendous amount of gratitude and obligation.

Below: The Castle Burgoyne on Beach Street, about 1940.

First, he built a new home, the Castle Burgoyne, right in the middle of town. The turreted mansion, its stable and grounds occupied the largest block in downtown Daytona, from Volusia Avenue to Bay Street, and employed a good portion of the citizenry in its construction. And that was not the end of his one-man public works campaign. He was a charter member of the Halifax River Yacht Club and put up the money for construction of the clubhouse, which extended into the Halifax River along riparian rights donated by Laurence Thompson. A year after those projects were completed, he commissioned a 75-foot yacht from the Daytona Boat Yards. Again, so many men were employed in its construction that a school holiday was declared the day she was launched. The whole town lined the riverbank and cheered as the Sweetheart—his pet name for his wife Mary—made her way up to the boathouse in front of Castle Burgoyne. A grateful town would always call him "Commodore" after that.

When Burgoyne arrived in Daytona, the area had outgrown its days as a pioneer village but was still something short of a city. With fewer than 2,000 people, it was nevertheless the largest community on the Halifax, though most of the towns and cities that surround it today were around then, too. Port Orange had been settled in its present location in 1872 and would be incorporated in 1913. The town of Blake, later South Daytona, had been settled in 1877. Holly Hill was a settlement and would become an incorporated town at the turn of the century. But each of these towns had its own local economy; Daytona was not the hub it would become in a few short years.

Two views of downtown Daytona at the turn of the century, an era dominated by Charles Burgoyne. Bicycles were the common mode of transport and narrow wooden bridges connected the peninsula to the mainland.

In fact, Daytona was struggling. Citrus had brought the first settlers, but hard freezes, tropical storms and the slow development of rail transportation had decimated one crop after another. When the railroads did come, they brought a new wave of immigration. But the completion of the tracks left many more people underemployed or out of work altogether.

Development of a winter tourist season was vital, but Daytona had problems there, as well. The city could boast of "easy access" to the resort communities of Seabreeze and Daytona Beach, but until the great consolidation of the 1920s, Daytona would not have a presence on the beachside. As it was, the most prosperous business in town was Bill Jackson's General Store, and the key to his success was a boat that allowed him to move merchandise all the way to Hobe Sound. When Pinewood Cemetery was built on the beachside, city fathers were confidant the resting souls therein would never be bothered by urban growth from Daytona, much less Bike Week and the Boothill Saloon.

Florida in general, as a former state in the Confederacy, had an image problem to overcome. People did not speak of Southern hospitality in those days. Instead, most Americans viewed Southerners, including those in Florida, as a lawless, depraved breed of humanity, an image formed by such popular and romantic novels as Uncle Tom's Cabin. The author of that book, Harriet Beecher Stowe, would express surprise on her first visit to Florida that the people were as law abiding as any in New England where she had lived most of her life. But she would also warn her readers that Florida did not live up to the "Paradise Regained" that Henry Flagler was trying to sell the public, and wealthy tourists were likely to be disappointed.

Stowe wrote:

> *Tourists generally come with their heads filled with romantic ideas of waving orange groves, flowers, fruits, all bursting forth in tropical abundance. What they find is a dead sandy level, with patches of rough coarse grass, and tall pine trees whose tops are so far in the air they cast no shade, and a little scrubby underbrush.*

Three views of the Halifax River Yacht Club: (above photo) as it looked in the 1890s, when Charles Burgoyne was the club's commodore; (middle photo) as it looked in the 1920s; (below) and as it looks today.

An accurate view of much of Florida, but not the luscious Halifax area—in those days, at least. When Burgoyne arrived in Daytona, bears, wildcats, even whole herds of deer still wandered along its banks. The river was completely unspoiled. Great schools of silver mullet would explode from the river when dolphins gave chase, scattering the sunlight in every direction. The sound made by thousands of fish slapping the water all at once left an impression few people were likely to forget. And shrimp were so plentiful that you could feed an entire family with just two or three casts of a net. It was a hunter's and fisherman's paradise.

What Daytona lacked was a Flagler hotel, with its guarantee of quality and luxury that made St. Augustine, Ormond and Palm Beach such attractive destinations. Daytona needed its own attractions, and a woman named Edith Newell was largely responsible for getting Burgoyne involved. Newell persuaded Burgoyne to fund, from his own pocket, a number of improvements to the city, all designed to make the city more attractive to wealthy tourists.

Burgoyne built the city's first real auditorium, the Casino Burgoyne, on the southeast corner of Beach Street and Orange Avenue, with a porch extending over the river. The Casino, built in the same turreted style as Castle Burgoyne, became a gathering place for wealthy winter tourists. Every year, Burgoyne paid the heady sum of $4,000 to have his favorite musicians, the Royal Italian Band under the direction of Rocco Saricina, give concerts three times a day at the Casino from January through May. In the off-season, the Casino was available to local residents and a favorite haunt for checker players.

Electricity came to Daytona in 1902, and Burgoyne lit Beach Street with white-way lighting, a necessary step before Daytona could attract the kind of nightspots rich people favored. Soon there were nightclubs like the Lido and three theaters screening the latest from Hollywood's silent stages.

With that kind of support, smaller luxury hotels began to flourish in Daytona and on the peninsula. The Princess Issena, the Clarendon, the Ridgewood, none of them were large enough when they opened to promote the kind of season-long activities sponsored by Flagler's Ormond Hotel—the fancy dress balls and tournaments and such. But a 70-room hotel became much more attractive if it was near a large auditorium and a thriving entertainment district.

Racing and speed trials played an important role in promoting the area. And Burgoyne played a prominent role in that as well, serving as president of the Florida East Coast Auto Club, which organized the events, and donating handsome prizes to the winners. He also paid for many of the street improvements that made the chauffeured excursions of rich folks more comfortable, and had the speed limit raised from 8 to 10 mph so those excursions weren't so interminable.

It was the first of the great tourism campaigns in Daytona's history, and it culminated in 1914 with the arrival of oil magnate John D. Rockefeller at the Clarendon Hotel for the winter season. Rockefeller would spend the remaining winters of his life in Ormond, first in Flagler's hotel, then in his own home, The Casements.

The Daytona Beach Municipal Airport at Bethune Point, 1931. The area's first airport was the beach, but when regular passenger service was added to airmail service, and the planes got bigger, the operation was moved across the river.

But the signal event of having the world's richest man come to Daytona had an incalculable effect on the city's reputation as a tourist destination.

Meanwhile, Charles and Mary Burgoyne lived like royalty in The Castle. In a great round room they entertained lavishly. The finest champagne flowed. Couples danced to Saricina's Royal Italian Band, or listened to complete Beethoven symphonies on Burgoyne's massive pipe organ, which he had rigged for automatic playing like a player piano. On the outside, townspeople heard the muffled organ or watched the silhouettes whirling in the stained glass windows. Children climbed trees for a glimpse above his high fence of the great man showing guests his horses. His parties, reputed to be on a scale as lavish as Tremalichio's, were another high point for the wealthy industrialists and financiers wintering in Florida. Invitations were sometimes sent to the local gentry, sometimes not. It bred more envy among the city's elite than among the common folk.

The Burgoynes remained popular with the working class. But among the leading merchants and businessmen of the day they developed a reputation for snobbery, and that led to a plot to humiliate Burgoyne by having him defeated for commodore of the yacht club. Publisher T. E. Fitzgerald got wind of it and tipped off Burgoyne, but it left a sour taste in everyone's mouth, particularly in Mary Burgoyne's, who was fiercely devoted to her husband.

It is no exaggeration to say that Daytona was built in the image of Charles Burgoyne. There are the obvious influences, like the turreted architecture that dominated the town during his era, and the immeasurable good done by his many contributions to area churches and needy families. Burgoyne died in 1916, at age 69.

The whole town turned out for his funeral in Pinewood Cemetery. Flags flew at half-staff. Mary marked his grave with a pedestal and a six-foot angel sculpted in Florentine marble. Then she went into seclusion at the Castle Burgoyne and few people ever saw her again. Stories began to circulate. The slip of a surgeon's knife during a face-lift had left her horribly disfigured. Or perhaps she had a rare skin disease. Apparently neither was true. She had been a poor girl when she married Burgoyne, not terribly sophisticated, and always loved him more than his money. When she was left with his money but not him, she became an easy target for shake-

The Casino Burgoyne on Beach Street, about 1920.

down artists. Soon the money was depleted, and she was left embittered and lonely, locked up in her Castle as it fell into disrepair. By the time she left it in the early 1940s, in the dead of night, to spend the remaining few years of her life in seclusion elsewhere, the great house had become an eyesore. Later it would be torn down to make way for new shopping venues.

Daytona has seen a lot of rich people since the days of Charles Burgoyne, some of them wealthier by far, but none his equal. He lived in an age of giants, and though he was a giant in just a very small corner of the world, he was able to thoroughly transform that corner. Time has eroded his influence, though. His Castle, his Navy, his Casino all gone, and the wealthy, his peers, no longer winter in Daytona Beach. Now and then you'll see a turret atop some edifice built years after his death and wonder if the architect was influenced by Burgoyne's hand in an earlier age of design. Maybe. Maybe not. For many years people celebrated his birthday in Daytona, but that has ended, too. In the 1950s, vandals tore down the angel his wife had mounted above his grave. Today, his name is hardly mentioned.

Two views of the Clarendon Hotel. At left, as it appeared in the late 19th century, and at right, as it appeared in the 1920s, when it was headquarters for Florida Land Boom speculators. Various fires caused the appearance of Daytona Beach's most historically significant hotel to change several times over the years. Today the hotel is the Holiday Inn Sunsplash on Atlantic Avenue and Seabreeze Boulevard. The old tunnel that provides beach access is part of the hotel dating back to the 1920s, as is the ballroom above it.

Jerome Burgman

If there was a best time to live and work along the Halifax, it probably fell between the end of World War II and the mid-1960s. Not the longest of epochs, those 20-odd years, but a kind of golden age, nonetheless, at least for the typical working family. People had survived a depression and won a war. Florida was booming again and employment was steady. Most families could own a home and afford a new car now and then. These weren't swank or elegant times, just good years to raise a family and live a real life. Best of all, Disney's big theme park was somewhere in California, and Daytona Beach was the best year-round vacation spot in Florida.

Summer tourism is taken for granted now. It has long replaced winter as the peak season in Central Florida, so it can be hard to imagine that someone actually had to think up the idea. Someone had to look at all those empty hotels and say: We could put people there, even in the middle of July.

That person was Jerome Burgman. He was a superb salesman, but the only thing he wanted to sell was Daytona Beach, which he thought was just about the best place on earth to be.

"The World's Most Famous Beach," he called it back in the 1920s, and the name stuck. "It's Cooler in Daytona Beach"—that was his, too.

He thought anyone could be happier in Daytona Beach, and devoted most of his life to proving it. He was a printer by trade, but could be thoroughly indifferent to his work for months at a time and his family jokes that he probably gave away more money than he ever made. He was a modest man, happiest when he was tramping alone through the woods with a camera, or sitting high on a dune, fleshing out his ideas with pencil and paper, or sharing a joke with lodge brothers from the Elks or Moose. But if you want to pinpoint the single most important day in the history of Daytona Beach since the railroads arrived, it was probably the day Burgman figured out a way to get rid of mosquitoes.

Salt marsh mosquitoes were the big problem in those days, had been since the first settlers arrived, probably since the first Indians. They could look like dinosaurs next to the little things that buzz around our ears today. And every year, like clockwork, they descended in April, just as the last rich folks were boarding their trains for the return trip north.

As a boy growing up in the coastal village of Seabreeze at the turn of the century, Burgman noticed that grownups were afraid of two things in the summer: the "tropical" sun and those big mosquitoes. Those were the days when everyone rode bicycles. Bicycles were as common as cars are today on Beach Street. But even in the dog days of August, people would be wheeling down the street in high, stiff collars, black alpaca coats and straw hats. Men and women both carried black cotton umbrellas, a final line of defense from the sun, and little fans that looked like a pony's tail to swat away mosquitoes.

The mosquitoes were more than a nuisance, of course. They carried malaria and yellow fever. The deadliest epidemics had ended when the local people discovered artesian wells and covered up their old open wells, a hazardous source of breeding. But that hadn't stopped the salt marsh mosquitoes—these didn't breed in town.

In 1904, when he was 19 years old, Jerome and his younger brother Leo opened their own print shop with the help of their father, Charles. It was a reasonable thing to do, seeing as how their grandmother, Helen Wilmans Post, was the author of twelve books and numerous pamphlets and thousands of mailings on the subject of Mental Science, an outgrowth of the teachings of the radical theologian Phineas Quimby. The major surviving thread of that 19th-century phenomenon is the Christian Science movement founded by Mrs. Post's cousin, Mary Baker Eddy. The Burgman brothers set up shop in the basement of Grandmother Helen's opera house, where she lectured the disciples of Mental Science who wintered at her resort community. The whole town of Seabreeze was a family affair. Relatives also owned the Princess Issena Hotel and The Colonnades, so between lecture programs, menus and mailings, there was enough work to keep the boys in business.

There was also a lot of downtime, though. Then Jerome and Leo would head out to the marshes around Thompson and Bulow Creeks, where they cut coquina rock with wire saws. Much of the coquina found today in old buildings and stone fences was cut by Jerome and Leo as boys. It was there that Jerome found the breeding ground for the salt marsh mosquitoes and figured that if you could drain the marshes for just a short time each April, the mosquito eggs would fail to hatch and the mos-

Two views of Daytona Beach in its heyday as Florida's most popular tourist destination, from about 1945 to 1965.

quito problem would be all but eliminated. But Jerome was just a youth, and that was an idea he had to file away for another day.

Seabreeze had been colonized by Jerome's grandparents, Helen and Colonel C. C. Post, two transplanted Californians. If Mathias Day had brought with him some notion that the city he founded would someday be proof of God's grace on earth, the Posts had him trumped in spades when it came to visions. They envisioned their town (which stretched from where Auditorium Boulevard is today, north to Golf Boulevard) as a world center of Mental Science. The opera house they built was to be the focus of cultural activity. A golf course was built on Golf Boulevard, about where Ortona Elementary School is today, and a Mental Science university was planned for University Boulevard, where Our Lady of Lourdes church now stands.

Jerome Burgman, the man who created summer tourism in Daytona Beach, at his office, a place he was rarely seen when he was alive. Burgman was happiest when he was either alone with nature or out promoting Daytona Beach as the perfect destination.

The Posts never lived to see their dream fulfilled. The fact is, their unorthodox treatment of the New Testament offended many people, and their dyed-in-the-wool abolitionist views ran contrary to the rising tide of racial segregation that began to overwhelm the Daytona area early in the 20th century. Eventually, Mrs. Post found herself on trial in a federal courtroom in Jacksonville, charged with mail fraud for accepting donations in exchange for promises that she would share a daily minute of meditation with the subscriber, no matter where that person was on the planet. The jury decided she had promised more minutes than there were in a day and found her guilty. The judge, for reasons no longer discernible, took issue with either the jury or the prosecution, fined her a few dollars and sent her on her way. But both Helen and her husband were left broken by the experience and died a few short years later, within months of one another.

In any case, their devotion to Mental Science never took root with the rest of their family, and the town of Seabreeze became a much more conventional resort town. Finally, in 1925 Jerome's extended family of Burgmans, Posts, Powers and Baggetts decided to support Daytona's plans to consolidate with Seabreeze and Daytona Beach to create the larger city of Daytona Beach.

This was the time of the big land boom, when speculators crowded the Clarendon Hotel, making and losing fortunes in a day. Undeveloped lots in unplanned subdivisions sold for as much as $11,000, not much less than an undeveloped beachside lot sells for today. J. Saxton Lloyd, the car dealer, used to tell a story that illustrates just how wild the land boom was. In the summer before his senior year of high school, Lloyd was working for a few dollars a week behind the counter of the Daytona Beach Pier with his best friend, Buddy Ebson, who would later move to Hollywood and a career as a "Beverly Hillbilly." Another boy convinced Lloyd to quit his job and pay a couple of dollars for a real estate license. He did, and in his first week agreed to acquire a property for a New York investor headquartered at The Clarendon. One deal. All Lloyd had to do was act as an errand boy. He made $2,000. A small fortune in those days, more money than his family had ever seen at one time. He decided not to tempt fate and quit the business after that one deal, and in the fall returned to high school and his paper route.

He probably imagined, like a lot of people did, that the boom could go on forever. The backers of consolidation had dreams of creating a true metropolis on the Halifax, but Ormond Beach, Holly Hill and South Daytona all opted out of the proposed government. Port Orange, stranded on the other side of South Daytona, wanted in but couldn't. So the metropolis never happened and the Halifax area remained a splintered collection of seaside and riverside communities.

Above: The Florida East Coast Auto Club at the turn of the century.

Then, the bottom dropped out of the land boom and the Great Depression hit in quick succession. Hotels struggled to stay open and the smaller guest homes closed their doors. As a boy, Burgman had stood on the wooden bridges crossing the Halifax and seen schools of mullet so thick it seemed to him that he could walk across them from one shore to the other. Now there were so many men trying to feed their families with casting nets that the mullet and shrimp began to thin out, never to return in those numbers.

It was during this period that Burgman found himself drawn into public life. It was a natural step for him. Just about everyone in his family had served in some government post in the old town of Seabreeze. His father, Charles, had made a larger impact as president of the Daytona Beach Chamber of Commerce. It was Charles Burgman who got the Florida legislature to approve dredging in the Halifax in 1927, opening the Intracoastal Waterway. Soon, about 85 percent of the navigation on the river was devoted to pleasure boating, increasing the tourist trade.

Jerome Burgman would follow his father as a Chamber president. He also held numerous posts in the Lions, Elks, Moose and other civic organizations. His résumé might have made him look like little more than a knee-jerk joiner, but that belies the real importance those groups played in the Daytona Beach of that era. This, after all, was the heyday of the political bosses—Jim Titus, Bert Fish and Francis Whitehair—lining their pockets and doling out favors, but accomplishing little in the way of effective government.

Into that breach stepped men like Burgman and Lloyd; Ucal Cunningham of the Cunningham Oil Company; Billy Baggett, who ran the Ocean Park Hotel; Clyde Morris, the druggist; and Father William Mullally at St. Paul's. Whether it was lending Mary Bethune enough money to keep her struggling school open, or finding a job for someone about to lose his home, these men and others like them kept Daytona Beach afloat during the long years of vote buying and influence peddling.

Below: The town of Seabreeze as it looked about the time of consolidation.

Probably the most useless thing Burgman ever did was win a race for the City Commission. That was during the Ed Armstrong years, and throughout his two-year term, Burgman found himself on the losing end of a long string of four-to-one votes.

It was during this same time, though—the mid-1930s—that Burgman created mosquito control in Daytona Beach. He headed up a citizens committee that roped in enough state and federal dollars to experiment with his idea of briefly draining the marshes in April. The summer infestations eased and the road was cleared for summer tourism.

Summer tourism became Burgman's passion. For years, warm winters had been the foundation of the Halifax economy. Burgman hoped that ocean breezes could work the same magic in the summer. Air-conditioning wasn't common, and the few degrees of coolness those ocean breezes brought Daytona Beach became his selling point.

The idea was to make Daytona Beach a destination for anyone a day's drive away. The hotels and guest cottages would then drop their prices for these working-family tourists. Burgman and his lodge brothers would load the municipal band onto a flatbed truck, drive to Orlando, or Sanford, even Atlanta, and roll down some major thoroughfare in the dead of summer, the band playing and the men holding up signs with slogans like "It's Cooler in Daytona Beach," and "2,000 Cottages on the Beach." He targeted textile plants in North Carolina, where management required the workers (most of them young women working for low wages) to take their vacations the same two weeks each summer. These women never got much of a vacation until Burgman rolled into town and convinced them that in groups of four or six they could afford to all pile into a car and share a guest cottage in Daytona Beach for a couple of weeks.

The Daytona Beach Municipal Band used to give regular concerts downtown at, later, the Bandshell. Jerome Burgman found another use for the musicians. He would load them on a flatbed truck, drive to nearby cities and have the band play during rush-hour traffic while he and other community leaders held up signs saying "It's Cooler in Daytona Beach."

He called it "ad blitzing." In truth, it did some good, but didn't turn the economy around overnight. There was still the Depression, after all, and then a war. Wartime gas rationing put even Daytona Beach out of reach for most Southern workers. But Burgman showed that ad blitzing could work.

The most important thing he did was sell the local citizenry on the idea of summer tourism. "We're all in the tourism business whether we like it or not," Burgman told people. "All our livelihoods depend on bringing the tourists here."

With public support behind him, an advertising tax district was created and Burgman directed its efforts for more years than he cared to think about. Bandwagon blitzing gave way to print promotions featuring frolicking young ladies on the beach. A kind of wholesome sexuality became the selling point for Daytona Beach, and eventually, the whole nature of the Halifax region began to change. Wealthy winter tourists, arriving by train with steamer trunks packed for the season, began to vanish, especially with the development of commercial aviation. The "jet set" after all, could reach Saint-Tropez about as easily as Daytona Beach. They were replaced by what Burgman called "suitcase tourists," families or young singles arriving for a long weekend or a summer vacation. Mom, Dad, the kids, all playing on the beach by day, then at night taking strolls in the cool evening breeze along the Boardwalk, eating hot dogs and hamburgers, blowing a few pennies at an arcade, then catching the nightly concerts at the Bandshell.

For the first time in Daytona Beach's history, employment became steady. Hotels stayed open year-round. Once again, Daytona Beach had become a premier destination.

Burgman, perhaps more than any other person, is responsible for Daytona Beach as it exists today. It is worth noting that by the time he died in 1972 at age 89, he was not entirely pleased with his creation. His son, Donald, who still operates Burgman Printing, today the oldest business in Daytona Beach, says that his father deeply regretted the assault on nature that was part of overdevelopment.

Jerome had done everything he could to have people come to Daytona Beach, but it wasn't a spigot that could simply be turned off. As Donald tells it, his father really had no religion except a love for nature, and his chief regret in his old age was that so much of the region's natural beauty had been razed and buried by development. His last years in public life were devoted to preserving some small part of the Halifax's native beauty in public parks. He helped to create Tomoka State Park north of Ormond Beach and served on its advisory board until the board was eliminated. He was a proponent of parks throughout the region.

Also, Jerome had high hopes that the space age, which had brought such clean, high-tech enterprises as Embry-Riddle Aeronautical University, Martin Marietta and Hudson Tool and Die to Volusia County, would prove to be the next great economic boon. But Burgman died six months to the day before America launched Apollo 17, the last of the manned lunar missions, effectively ending the great boom in high-tech development in Florida. But he did live long enough to see Disney World open in Orlando, an event that would siphon off much of the local tourist trade, gradually pushing Daytona Beach toward the middle of the pack as a tourist destination.

Overall, Burgman's contributions were significant and positive. He remains one of the key figures in the history of the Halifax area—a man whose ideas helped shape it for the better. His greatest contribution, according to Donald, wasn't the sort of thing people raise statues to. It was his interest in people and his eagerness to get individuals involved with the betterment of the city. Daytona Beach is filled today with people who recall some story of his great generosity. Good citizenship. Community spirit. Quaint, archaic virtues, that Jerome Burgman made a cornerstone of modern Daytona Beach.

When he died, the local paper summed up his contributions with these words: *"The shortcomings of Daytona Beach could be ascribed to the fact that it has had too few Jerome Burgmans."*

Embry-Riddle Aeronautical University

Embry-Riddle Aeronautical University is unique in the annals of academia—a university devoted solely to aeronautics and aerospace. This high-tech enterprise can trace its roots to the barnstorming days in the 1920s, when bi-plane pilot John Paul Riddle left behind him the thrill circus of acrobatic aviation and became one of the first air jockeys to realize that the future of commercial aviation depended on safety and reliability, not seat-of-the-pants heroics. With his friend, student and financier, T. Higby Embry, he started the Embry-Riddle Company and began to teach the most rigorous piloting course available anywhere.

Headquartered in Dade County, Embry-Riddle trained 26,000 British and American pilots, mechanics and technicians during World War II. In the mid-1960s the institute faced extinction when the Dade County Port Authority decided to close the Tamiami Airport where the school was located. The school began to look for a place to relocate and settled on Daytona Beach, where there was lots of open air space and a civic leadership hungry for growth.

So hungry, in fact, that community leaders, led by the Jaycees and the Committee of 100, rounded up hundreds of trucks and vans from every business in town that could spare them for a weekend and created a most unusual convoy. The entire school—every piece of paper, library book, desk, lamp, whatever—made its way from Miami to Daytona on that convoy. The savings to the school was in the hundreds of thousands of dollars. The benefit to the community was inestimable. Since 1965, Embry-Riddle has grown from a training school into a fully accredited university of 5,000 students with a second residential campus in Arizona.

Big Bill France

For fifty years, Bill France, Sr., strode the Halifax like a colossus. If his name is not known by everyone—and it very nearly is—his legacy certainly is, and his influence is unavoidable. He was a strong man, in mind, body and spirit. So strong, in fact, that he seemed to warp Daytona Beach into his own image simply by being there. And it is fair to say that Daytona Beach is what it is today because that's the way he left it.

Three views of Spring Break. Clean-cut collegians in 1964 (below). Fun and sun from the "Brady Bunch" era (top right), when the city began to promote Spring Break heavily. Spring break in 1991, when the crush of youths became so great local promoters sent MTV packing and started to scale back (bottom right).

France's development of the Daytona International Speedway and his elevation of stock car racing to a national sport is the greatest success story to emerge in the annals of business in the Halifax region. It grew from a love of cars and racing that seemed to be inborn.

Certainly it was there when he was 16 years old. That was in the late 1920s and France was still living in his hometown of Washington, D.C. There was nothing unusual about him asking his father to borrow the family car, a Ford Model T. His dad didn't mind. What his dad didn't know, though, was that young Bill would drive it to Laurel, Maryland, and race it on the 48-degree banking of the mile and an eighth board track there. Young Bill tried to get it to stay up there on that banking but the old thing just didn't have the power. It kept sliding down. And when Bill's father took it back to the dealer, complaining that the tires kept wearing out, young Bill just didn't say a word.

Like Charles Burgoyne and Jerome Burgman, France never finished high school. After two years he quit and went to work in a garage. By 1934 he had a wife, Annie, and a son, Bill, Jr. And he'd had about all he wanted of working in the snow. So with a car, a trailer, some tools and $25 in cash, the France family set off for Florida, where he figured at least it would be warm beneath the cars he had to fix.

"The first time I saw Daytona Beach I thought it was the prettiest place I'd ever seen," he once said in an interview. "It was a perfect fall day, the tide was out and the beach was deserted."

Pretty enough to stay, apparently. Big Bill, as he would always be known—he stood six-foot-five—got a job as a mechanic at Sax Lloyd's Beach Street Buick dealership, and the family settled into a tiny one-bedroom house.

To this point, there's nothing in France's story to set him apart from any of the thousands of young men who brought their families to Daytona Beach in the 1920s and 1930s. What gave destiny a nudge was Malcolm Campbell's decision to move his speed trials from Daytona Beach to the Salt Flats of Utah in 1935. Campbell wanted to break the 300 mph mark behind the wheel of his Bluebird, but the beach surface was too rough because of tides, the wind too unpredictable.

Daytona had become "The World's Most Famous Beach" chiefly on the publicity generated by the speed trials. The city wanted something to replace them, so they first turned to race promoter Sig Haugdahl, who had the idea for a racecourse on the beach and the adjacent highway. The Beach Road Course, as it became known, was

DAYTONA BEACH
RECREATION DEPT
WELCOME COLLEGIANS
FREE FRISBEES!

to carve out its own legend, but not on the basis of the first race in 1936. The race was designed to be a handicap. Cars left in reverse order of their finish in time trials, so the fastest of the 27 cars started the race more than half an hour after the slowest. The whole thing was a mess. There were two turns on the mile-and-a-half course, and the cars just tore them up. The race had to be called far short of the 250 miles intended. The whole event just collapsed in utter confusion. France, driver of a '35 Ford, was later told he'd come in fifth, but was never able to determine just how the judges decided that. Not that it mattered much. France took home $300 for his finish, a welcome sum in the days when minimum wage paid about $14 a week.

Bill France, center, in the 1950s, at the site where he would build his speedway.

The city lost $22,000 on that race and dropped out of the racing business. In 1937, the Elks Club took over. They lost money, too. In 1938, a delegation from the Chamber of Commerce went to visit France in his Main Street garage, a sort of headquarters for all the local barrel and dirt track racers. They asked if he knew anyone interested in putting on a race that year. As it turned out, France would organize the race, and a local restaurant owner, Charlie Reese, would put up the money. That year, France and Reese sold 5,000 tickets at fifty cents a piece and turned a profit of $250. The next year they raised the price to a dollar, sold the same amount of tickets, and cleared more than $2,000. France had already learned his first important lesson about promoting races.

For the next 20 years France would promote beach races of one sort or another. People have fond memories of those times, but in truth, beach racing was not as unique as many seem to think. Jacksonville, St. Augustine, New Smyrna Beach, Cocoa Beach—these and other seaside cities and towns all had beach racing at the time. Granted, they were barrel races on shorter courses—the Daytona Beach route would eventually be more than four miles long—but the whole phenomenon of beach racing was on a par with dirt tracks. Stock cars had none of the glamour and prestige that Indy cars or grand prix racing had. Just good old boys with their souped-up cars, that was the image of stock cars.

France had no trouble making a living. By the late 1940s he was one of the top promoters in the South. When he wasn't too busy promoting, he'd race the cars himself. And when he wasn't racing, he was often inserting his six-foot, five-inch frame between two feuding drivers, restoring civility. If France had done nothing more with his life, he would still be a dirt track legend. But at age 38, he was just about to start his life's real work.

France knew in 1947 that stock car racing had a long way to go before it could reach the major leagues of motor sports. He started by identifying three things it needed right away.

First, he wanted to get rid of the sneaky promoters and the frequent after-race squabbling that marred the sport. He wanted some kind of organization to make

Three views of beach racing. Bill France created a combination beach and road raceway in the 1930s and continued to run races there until the 1950s, when he opened his super-speedway.

rules and keep records. The record keeping was important. He wanted a point system so drivers could win points at different tracks, with some kind of purse at the end of a season. If you wanted drivers to develop name recognition, gather a following, you had to have some kind of champion, and a statistical champion was the kind France wanted. Americans loved statistics. Boys who had never seen Ted Williams or Joe DiMaggio play baseball could recite their stats from heart. France wanted champions who would become household names. Over the years, he would cultivate the image of drivers—from Junior Johnson and Glenn "Fireball" Roberts to Richard Petty, Cale Yarborough and Bobby Allison—as if they were products of the Hollywood studio system.

Next, he wanted to keep the cars technically uniform. The drivers would be the stars, not some high-compression heads. He also wanted to stick with American-made cars. British and German automakers had long dominated racing, but in those days Americans didn't drive foreign cars for the most part. They drove Chevys, Pontiacs and Fords, and France figured the fan in the stands would feel he had a greater stake in the race if his own model was down there on the track.

And finally, he wanted some protection for the drivers. The cars should be as safe as possible, but the drivers themselves needed insurance, because accidents were always going to be a part of auto racing.

The end result of all this was that a week before Christmas in 1947, France gathered some of the best men in stock car racing to a meeting room at the Streamline Hotel and laid out his vision of what stock car racing could become. That convocation proved to be the birth of NASCAR—the National Association for Stock Car Auto Racing—today a multibillion dollar enterprise and the single most significant source of fame and recognition for Daytona Beach.

Two years later, stock car racing took another giant step forward with construction of the first super-speedway in Darlington, South Carolina. France had been lobbying city leaders for such a speedway in Daytona Beach, and Darlington gave him the final edge he needed. For the next ten years, the design and construction of the Daytona International Speedway would become the focus of his energies.

The Daytona International Speedway under construction in the 1950s.

His concept was revolutionary—a 2.5-mile track with two 48-degree banked turns, "as steep as they could lay asphalt," was his goal, and a dogleg bend at the finish line. He wanted the excitement of cars banking as high as possible, with flat turns so the cars could run in more than one groove and pass as easily as in the straightaways.

The first running of the Daytona 500, an event every bit as important to the area's history as the records set by W. K. Vanderbilt and Malcolm Campbell, came on February 22, 1959. Lee Petty was the winner, inching out Johnny Beauchamp at the finish line, but the results weren't known until three days after the race, when films and photographs sent to New York for development returned.

The speedway put Daytona Beach back on the map to stay. France ruled both the speedway and NASCAR with an iron hand. His development of a second super-speedway in Talladega, Alabama, in 1969 extended his control of the sport even further. Along the way he became friends with Alabama Governor George Wallace. France even headed Wallace's Florida campaign in the 1972 Democratic presidential primaries. Wallace was a surprise winner in the race.

A running of the Daytona 500 in the 1980s.

The first race at Talladega provided a fine display of France's management style. NASCAR drivers, led by Richard Petty, boycotted the race, protesting that the track wasn't safe. To break what amounted to a strike, France recruited unknown drivers and put fans in the seats by promising the ticket stubs would be good for free admissions for future races

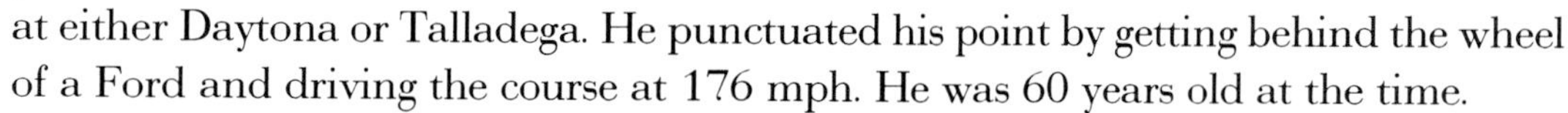

at either Daytona or Talladega. He punctuated his point by getting behind the wheel of a Ford and driving the course at 176 mph. He was 60 years old at the time.

Over the years he also fought off challenges to his authority from the Teamsters union, the Big Three automobile manufacturers and other speedway owners. He was sometimes called a tyrant, but mere tyranny was never his aim. France shouldered the burden of raising stock car racing's profile, making it profitable everywhere and challenging Indianapolis racing for popularity. He did it by controlling every nuance of the sport. He was even accused of ordering yellow flags to create dramatic finishes in races that would have been effectively won many laps before the finish line—a charge that always made him bristle.

France retired from his various posts with NASCAR and the speedway in 1972, turning management of the day-to-day affairs over to his son, Bill France, Jr. He didn't really need titles to remain the dominant figure in stock car racing until ill health overtook him in the 1980s. He died of Alzheimer's disease in 1992. At his funeral, a checkered flag covered the coffin.

His impact on the local economy and local culture was nearly incalculable. The yearly cycle of Speed Weeks every February leading up to the Daytona 500, the Daytona 200 motorcycle race in March, and the Pepsi 400 in July established the rhythm for the entire Halifax area from the mid-1960s on. The hotels and motels from Interstate 95 to Highway A1A fill and empty according to a calendar Bill France drew up nearly a generation ago.

Bill France was singularly unconcerned with history. He bought Malcolm Campbell's Bluebird, then left it in a warehouse for years. He never opened a NASCAR museum, making it virtually the only sports-governing body in the nation without one. Only after his death did the France family commission a statue of Bill Sr. and Annie. The Daytona USA exhibit did not open until four years after his death. That lack of concern about his legacy is not unusual for a man of action, which Bill France certainly was. He was not someone to brood over history, especially since he was willing to change it on a moment's notice.

GATEWAY
WORLD'S MOST FAMOUS BEAC
MAIN ST.
LOWENBRAU
STOP
RED

Partners in Progress

The Daytona Beach/Halifax area is at a crossroads today, just as it has been throughout its history. Its future is in the hands of a new generation of residents, many of whom have migrated here in hopes of building a better future for their families and businesses.

Many community leaders want to see not only tourism improved, but more diversification in the economy and a stronger, more stable industrial base. The one refrain heard from community leaders again and again is the yearning for someone to step up with the ideas and imagination to lead, and perhaps that is where the future really lies, in the imagination of another Mathias Day or John Anderson or Jerome Burgman.

Left: Daytona Beach adopted Jerome Burgman's slogan—"The World's Most Famous Beach"—for many years.

There is a good chance that you will here from that person in this chapter, what might be called the living history of the region. The preceding chapters have told the story of Daytona Beach through various voices—from Ernst d'Erlach to James Ormond to Bill France. Those are the voices of the past. Now you will hear the voices of the present and the future.

The profiles in this chapter were prepared by business profile writer Barbara Johnson with the direct involvement of the subjects. These individuals and corporations are the sponsors of this books, and we are greatly indebted to them for their participation.

If you live in the Daytona Beach area, these are your neighbors, and this is a chance to know them better. But they are also more—they are community leaders. Each of these profiles is a success story, though the goals are often quite different. It is through these goals—the dreams of the men and women who live among us—that the present has taken shape. The future awaits.

Daytona Beach/ Halifax Area Chamber of Commerce

Above: In simpler times, a Chamber of Commerce advertising campaign featured bathing beauties and the slogan, It's cooler in Daytona Beach.

Below: The old Burgoyne Casino located at the corner of Beach Street and Orange Avenue was home to the Chamber in the 1920's.

A great Chamber of Commerce advertising campaign used to mean posing bathing beauties around an oversized thermometer under the slogan *It's cooler in Daytona Beach.*

Back when Daytona was the newly crowned ***World's Most Famous Beach,*** a group of businessmen on a mission from the Chamber could even drum up business by dressing in women's bathing suits and making a spectacle of themselves in Georgia and Alabama.

Today, tourism is an industry as competitive and sophisticated as any other. As the business has evolved, so has the Daytona Beach/Halifax Area Chamber of Commerce.

The Chamber campaigns of the 1990s feature urban planners and venture capitalists, task forces and public forums, all with a common goal: to develop a new vision for the Daytona Beach/Halifax area, and to marshal the community's resources to turn the vision into reality. Through its own initiative, and at the request of local government, the Chamber has assumed the role of consensus builder to guide the community toward a more prosperous future.

The Chamber's journey from chief booster to long-range strategist spans more than three-quarters of a century. Organized in 1919, the Chamber began with a budget of $200 and a promise to "insure more effective advertising." Over time, as the Chamber's interests expanded, the group was a major force behind the creation of a city marina on the Intracoastal Waterway and the relocation of Embry-Riddle Aeronautical University from Miami to Daytona Beach.

Now in its 77th year, the Chamber represents 1,100 member companies of all types. It is one of a small percentage of chambers nationwide accredited by the Chamber of Commerce of the United States.

Under the leadership of board chairman Bill Olivari and president George Mirabal, the Chamber operates under the conviction that residents and business people—its members—are, or should be, masters of the community's destiny. That pro-active stance has resulted in some major successes, and some undertakings with enormous potential.

One success story is the metamorphosis of Bike Week which is now touted as the largest motorcycle event in the world - and by far the most profitable event in the city.

In 1988, the Chamber accepted this challenge from the city: improve Bike Week in both ***quality*** and ***quantity***. A Chamber task force went to work, first promoting Bike Week as a festival in magazines that cater to the law-abiding biker, then raising the standards of vendors who set up shop along Main Street.

Today, half a million bikers come to the Halifax area for Bike Week, spending $280 million. The "average" attendee is a 42-year-old male with a $66,500 household income, and many are professionals or small business owners who bring along their wives. Residents who used to fear Bike Week now join in the festivities.

The Chamber's transformation of Bike Week became a model for the city. In 1989, after residents marched on City Hall to protest an out-of-control Spring Break, another Chamber task force was called upon to manage the event.

Perhaps the Chamber's most ambitious undertaking is "Take Part II," what the Chamber describes as an action plan to re-invent the tourism industry in the Daytona Beach/Halifax Area. The plan's name derives from the effort to involve the entire community in reshaping itself. The "action" in the plan is no less than a blueprint for redeveloping the core beach business district.

Begun in 1994 with $400,000 raised in just six weeks from private business, individuals and local government, Take Part II remains a work in progress. But progressing it is. Consultants have reached the point of producing detailed feasibility plans for the creation of water parks and other modern family amusements to entice investors to the beach. And through the cooperation of city government, 278 acres have been rezoned as an entertainment/recreation district to clear the way for redevelopment.

The underlying philosophy of today's Chamber is that neither the private sector nor the public sector can accomplish much of significance alone. But with the Chamber helping to bridge the two, the synergy can lead to something great.

Below: The Chamber moved into its current home on the intracoastal waterway in 1986. Here, a professional staff of 10 represents 1,100 member companies.

Jiloty Communications

Above: The Job Fair is improving the image and tone of Spring Break in Daytona Beach, Here, Mike Jiloty, who helped create the event, interviews a visiting college student for a job.

Below: Mike Jiloty and his staff of communications professionals headquartered in Holly Hill handle clients throughout Florida and in Colorado.

It was the kind of publicity money can't buy: a feature story in the *Wall Street Journal* portraying Spring Breakers in Daytona Beach as a serious bunch who apply for jobs with major corporate recruiters in between volleyball events and pool parties. Civic leaders have wrestled for years with the images that Spring Break evokes, with a distinct preference for an image of good, clean fun over a party image. They couldn't have drawn a more flattering portrait of Spring Break if they had written the article themselves.

And for Mike Jiloty, whose business it is to polish the area's image, the article was something of a coup. It proved to be a catalyst for nationwide coverage in daily newspapers, network television and on-line media.

As president of Jiloty Communications, located in the SunTrust Building, 1510 Ridgewood Avenue in Holly Hill, Jiloty presented the Career Fair concept to tourism officials in 1995. It quickly caught on with college students and, perhaps more importantly, with the *Wall Street Journal* and other major media. The hope is that the publicity will attract more responsible Spring Breakers and present a more wholesome image of the area to family visitors, the kind of tourists the area covets.

Jiloty lists the Career Fair as among his firm's most successful projects, and there have been many high profile campaigns over the company's 16-year history.

In 1980, the former advertising director for a savings and loan joined with local artist Jim Shipley and established the company as Jiloty, Shipley & Associates. The firm quickly established itself as a leader among advertising agencies in the Halifax area, and within a year had wrestled the local tourism bureau account from Florida's largest agency. Among the campaigns the firm developed for the tourism bureau was the *Just for the fun of it* campaign that ran for several years.

Later, the firm developed the inaugural marketing campaigns for the Ocean Center and the Volusia County Business Development Corporation. It helped pioneer tourism marketing on-line when it helped place Spring Break on the World Wide Web in 1994, a move that was written up in *USA Today* along with on-line efforts of the Super Bowl and Mardi Gras.

In 1986, Jiloty bought out his partner and expanded the competitive arena to include all of Florida with an occasional trek outside the state. Today, his enterprise includes affiliations with Harwell & Jiloty Marketing in Lakeland and Harwell, Jiloty and Metts in Colorado Springs.

Jiloty Communications itself has grown from three to twelve full time people with a full stable of freelance support. The firm represents about fifteen major clients and an equal number of smaller clients. The goal of the firm is to continue to expand its regional presence in the competitive advertising industry.

Museum of Arts and Sciences

The cultural heart of Daytona Beach is the Museum of Arts and Sciences, whose $10 million collection of art and artifacts is ranked among the top five in Florida.

Tucked midway between the entertainments of "the world's most famous beach" and the roar of the Speedway, the museum quietly goes about its business, exhibiting and interpreting objects of national and international import, enriching the lives of residents, guests, and children.

Over four decades, the lifeblood of the museum has been a continuous flow of bequests from Florida and national collectors, as well as generous public and private support.

The museum has gained a reputation beyond the borders of Florida in five important areas:

Masterworks of American Art, a collection of furniture, paintings, silver, and decorative arts from the days of the Pilgrims through the early twentieth century, has been called "breathtakingly beautiful" by *Florida Today*.

The Cuban Museum, a permanent exhibition of the most complete and artistically valuable collection of Cuban Fine and Folk Art outside of Cuba, is an important cultural resource for the millions of Cubans living in the United States.

Africa: Life and Ritual, a large collection of Sub-Saharan tribal and ritual objects, is included on the "African Heritage Trail," which explores African-American cultural roots. A must-see are 130 rare Ashante gold ornaments.

The Bouchelle Center for the Study of International Decorative Arts contains one of the largest and most important collections of its kind, with over 5,000 objects in silver, glass, semi-precious materials, and enamel.

The Prehistory of Florida gallery, a Pleistocene fossil collection from the Daytona Beach Bone Bed, includes the impressive thirteen-foot high skeleton of the giant ground sloth, the most complete example of this animal ever found in North America. This exhibition is a favorite with children of all ages.

Finally, the museum offers planetarium shows, many different temporary exhibitions from its own and other museum collections, lectures and workshops, videos, concerts, family programs, and nature trail tours. It occupies 65,000-square feet within the ninety-acre Tuscawilla Park Preserve. It publishes award-winning art books and a magazine. Its store offers original art, jewelry, small artifacts, scientific toys, and many other attractive items. Whether you can spend a few hours or a few days, the museum is the place not to miss.

The Museum of Arts and Sciences

1040 Museum Blvd., Daytona Beach, Florida 32114 • Phone (904) 255-0285

KEY

Information
Galleries
Museum Store
Rest Rooms
Museum Staff
Center for Florida History
Changing Exhibitions
Permanent Collections

NORTH WING
WEST WING
EAST WING
North Entrance and Parking
South Entrance and Parking

• Gallery Guide •

1. Lobby / Reception Desk
2. Root Hall Gallery
3. Chapman Root Hall Auditorium
4. The Cuban Museum
5. The Karshan Center of Graphic Art
6. Sculpture Court
7. The Museum Store
8. Planetarium
9. Africa: Life and Ritual
10. Prehistory of Florida
11. Science Gallery
12. Corridor Gallery
13. Ford Exhibitions Gallery
14. The Dow Gallery of American Art
15. Schulte Gallery of Chinese Art
16. The Bouchelle Gallery
17. Bouchelle Center for the Study of International Decorative Arts
18. Window in The Forest

HOURS OF OPERATION

TUES. - FRI. 9:00 a.m. - 4:00 p.m.

SAT. - SUN. 12:00 noon - 5:00 p.m.

Above: 65,000 square feet of art, science, and Florida history.

Command Medical Products

Above: Command Medical Products, one of the nation's fastest growing privately held companies, employs 140 people at its Ormond Beach factory.

After a hard day on the job, workers at Command Medical Products in Ormond Beach can go home, flip on the television, and admire their handiwork on *E.R.* or *Chicago Hope*.

Command Medical so dominates the market for plastic tubing and certain other hospital supplies that most surgical patients and many people treated in emergency rooms will be poked or prodded by one or another of the company's products. Even if the hospital is actually a Hollywood sound stage.

Founded in 1987 by David Slick, Command Medical was named by *Inc.* magazine as one of the fastest growing privately held companies in the United States. Revenues in the first five years grew 1,600 percent, and to date have grown more than 5,000 percent.

Today, Command Medical Products is located in a 56,000-square-foot factory at 15 Signal Avenue in the Ormond Beach industrial park. The company employs 140 people, up from seven when the plant opened in 1987.

Slick attributes the company's phenomenal growth in part to timing: Command Medical was the first company to do contract manufacturing, assembly, and packaging of complete hospital-ready equipment—thus cutting down on overhead expenses—at a time when hospitals were under pressure to cut costs.

Command Medical is the primary manufacturer of two common medical devices: an assembly used for laparoscopic surgery, and a blood connection system used in open heart surgery that allows the patient to be re-transfused with his own blood.

Both devices make use of plastic tubes, and Command Medical's machines run twenty-four-hours-a-day, producing over fifty million feet of tubing a year. Enough to fill the needs of most hospitals and Hollywood producers, too.

ACT Corporation

Above: The ACT Corporation's main campus is located at 1220 Willis Avenue in Daytona Beach.

Below: Pinegrove is ACT's new crisis stablization unit and a "one-stop shopping" center where people can receive evaluation, treatment and referrals.

The Community Mental Health Centers Act is hardly a household phrase. And when you think of the Kennedy Administration, this 1963 legislation certainly doesn't eat up the history books like the Cuban missile crisis, the space program, or the Berlin Wall. But in the field of mental health, it was the most important public policy corner ever turned, and its effects are easy to measure in Volusia and Flagler counties.

Before the Community Mental Health Centers Act created local mental health centers across the country, hundreds of people from Volusia and Flagler were confined in state mental hospitals each year. These often included people suffering from autism, mental retardation, depression, and Alzheimer's. Today, even with the explosive growth of Florida's population, that number has dropped to about forty, and is restricted to the severely mentally ill who pose a threat to themselves or others. New generations of psychiatric drugs deserve a large part of the credit, but so does the availability of community mental health services provided by non-profit organizations such as Act Corporation, which began operation in 1965 as the Guidance Center.

Act is one of Volusia County's largest employers. Act offers a wide range of services, both inpatient and outpatient, for adults and children. Daycare programs for adults and seniors provide social and health-related activities for participants. And inpatient services are available to stabilize people experiencing crisis.

Perhaps the most important link in these services is Pinegrove, the access center at 1150 Red John Drive in Daytona Beach. Here you will find a kind of "one-stop shopping," where highly trained clinical access specialists assess, inform, and refer people to the appropriate service or network within the community.

Outpatient services include substance abuse counseling, short-term, problem-focused therapy, and psychiatric care, including prescription services.

Also included in outpatient services are partial hospitalization and day treatment programs which offer specialized care for senior citizens and people in need of closely supervised rehabilitation programs.

Inpatient services cover crisis stabilization units for both adults and children, emergency services for people in immediate danger to themselves and others, a short-term residential facility, community residences and a special facility for Department of Corrections inmates and others referred by law enforcement officials.

Youth services include the B.E.A.C.H. House for teens in immediate need of food, shelter, clothing and medical care. An outreach program for runaway and homeless youths specifically designed for the Daytona Beach resort area helps youngsters stay out of harm's way.

And these are only a handful of the specialized mental health services provided by the Act Corporation, which works to anticipate the mental health needs of every citizen in Volusia and Flagler counties.

Act is funded in part by the Florida Department of HRS, Corrections and Juvenile Justice, Counties of Volusia and Flagler as well as private donations, commercial and public insurance programs.

Glenn S. Ritchey has served as president of Hall-Ritchey Management Co. Inc. since 1985.

Hall-Ritchey Management Company

Hurricane Bertha bore down on Florida's east coast in July 1996. As Daytona Beach residents evacuated and the city prepared for the worst, car dealer Glenn Ritchey gathered up keys to the new trucks sitting on his lot and handed them over to the Daytona Beach police. Should the worst happen night or day, disaster workers were authorized to commandeer his inventory to help rescue the city.

Ritchey, and Hall-Ritchey Management Company, have a firm grip on the title of "largest new and used car dealer in Daytona Beach." Nevertheless, Ritchey measures success not just in terms of how many cars and trucks he sells, but in whether he personally makes a difference in the lives of his neighbors.

On both accounts, Ritchey can rest assured he has arrived.

More than twenty-five years ago, Hall-Ritchey made a commitment to become the largest volume dealer of new and used cars and trucks in Daytona Beach. The company has maintained that position.

In 1996, fellow Rotarians in Daytona Beach named Ritchey the *Rotarian of the Year*, an honor recognizing him for long community service that goes well beyond deploying his fleet in a bona fide city emergency.

The story of Hall-Ritchey Management Company can be traced back to 1967 when Jon E. Hall arrived in Daytona Beach as vice president and general manager of the local Chevrolet dealership. Hall immediately fell in love with the area's beauty and knew this was where he wanted to make his home.

A native of South Carolina, Hall had begun his automotive career in 1954 working as a salesman at a friend's Chevrolet dealership in Valdosta, Georgia. Hall went on to work at GM's Chevrolet Motor Division in Detroit, followed by ten years as a district manager for the Chevrolet Motor Division. As district manager, his territory extended from South Georgia to North Florida, which became a springboard for his move to Daytona Beach.

After working as vice president and general manager, Hall acquired the dealership and teamed up with his longtime friend, Glenn Ritchey, to form Hall-Ritchey Management Company, with Ritchey as both partner and general manager. Ritchey became president and chief executive officer in 1985.

Over the years, the company grew from a single dealership in Daytona Beach to a far-flung chain of as many as ten dealerships in three states, employing hundreds of people. Today, in Daytona Beach alone, more than 325 people work for five Hall-Ritchey dealerships spread from the 300- to the 900-block of Nova Road: Jon Hall Jeep/Eagle; Jon Hall Chevrolet/GEO; Jon Hall Honda; Saturn of Daytona; and the newest addition in Daytona, Jon Hall Chevrolet OK Used Car Supercenter.

Hall attributes the success of their company to a simple business philosophy: providing the best selection of products and services at the best prices and terms.

"I've always wanted the Jon Hall family of dealerships to have a professional image in the community—one operated with honesty and integrity," Hall says.

The payoff for Hall-Ritchey's commitment to the customer has been bigger than just return business from satisfied car buyers. Hall was granted one of the first six Honda dealerships in Florida, and the Hall-Ritchey team opened one of the nation's original Saturn dealerships.

"Saturn has always taken customer satisfaction very seriously. Unless your scores were high enough, a dealer would never even be considered for a Saturn store," Ritchey says.

And judging by what his colleagues in the business say about him, Ritchey's scores on customer satisfaction are to be envied. In 1993, his peers in the Florida Automobile Dealers Association nominated Ritchey for the *Time* magazine Quality Dealership Award in recognition of his community service, sales record, and leadership.

So well-regarded is he in the business nationally that he was elected chairman of the National Dealer Council for Chevrolet, and the board of directors of General Motors invited Ritchey to address it on the subject of dealer-factory relations.

By the continued expansion of their business in Daytona Beach and their high-level of community involvement, both Ritchey and Hall demonstrate their belief in and commitment to Daytona Beach.

Ritchey, an active member over the years of the United Way and numerous bank and hospital boards, now serves on the Daytona Beach Board of Adjustments and Steering Committee for Economic Development. After the recent shocking murder of another local civic leader, Alan Robertson, Ritchey joined forces with others to create a citizens' "Crime Stoppers" program. And in 1997, Ritchey will begin his term as president of the Daytona Beach Rotary Club.

Hall and Ritchey agree that, "The future for Daytona Beach looks brighter than ever."

Left: Jon E. Hall, chairman of Hall-Ritchey Management Co. Inc., moved to Daytona Beach in 1967 and fell in love with the city.

Below: With five dealerships in Daytona Beach, Glenn Ritchey, left, and Jon E. Hall are the area's largest volume dealers.

Black, Crotty, Sims, Hubka, Burnett, Birch And Samuels, L.L.P.

Above: Members of the firm, seated left to right: Marla Rawnsley, E. William Crotty and Kathleen Crotty. Standing left to right: Harold Hubka, Random Burnett, Donald Birch and G. Larry Sims.

Ask any Democratic politician you find and he'll tell you—if he's lucky—that the road he travels, even if it leads to the White House, passes through the corporate law firm of Black, Crotty and Sims.

In a modest suite of offices at 501 North Grandview Avenue, above a bank in an old section of town, senior partner E. William Crotty has earned his reputation as one of the Democratic Party's top fund raisers. In a never-ending series of small dinner and cocktail parties, Crotty, often joined by his partners, raises hundreds of thousands of dollars for his favored candidates, pulling more money per capita out of the Daytona Beach area than anyplace else in the nation.

The syndicated columnist Robert Novak, writing in a 1988 issue of ***Forbes,*** put Crotty among the first tier of political fundraisers, alongside such men as Armand Hammer, Bruce Gelb, Robert Mosbacher and Walter Shorenstein. Crotty has been involved in every Democratic presidential campaign since Jimmy Carter's in 1976. He has hosted fundraisers for twenty-six Democrats in the United States Senate, as well as numerous House members, and state and local office holders, including Governor Lawton Chiles.

In the era of post-Watergate election reform, when candidates are limited to individual contributions of $1,000, men like Crotty, who can rope in massive numbers of contributions, have replaced the moguls like Howard Hughes and Clement Stone who could finance candidates directly from their own deep pockets.

That kind of influence only comes with a solid record of achievement, and Black, Crotty, Sims, Hubka, Burnett, Birch and Samuels is one of the oldest, most successful law firms in Daytona Beach. It can count among its clients many of the Halifax area's largest businesses and financial institutions, such as NASCAR, the Daytona International Speedway, SunTrust Bank and the Halifax Medical Center.

The firm has deep roots in Daytona, going back to the Depression when the late David Black opened a law practice on the beach. Bill Crotty came to Daytona in 1958 and joined the Black firm in 1967. He quickly immersed himself in the local political scene, turning Daytona Beach into a popular stop on the campaign trail.

Today, the firm numbers seven lawyers, including three with masters of law in taxation. The firm maintains a large practice of general business law, and specializes in representing clients' interests in Daytona Beach, Tallahassee and Washington D.C.

Burgoyne Properties

It was 1941 and years since the widow Burgoyne had set foot outside the gothic Beach Street mansion people called The Castle. In her husband's day, Charles Burgoyne had set the finest table in town, as only the richest man in town possibly could. People saw plenty of Mary Burgoyne in those days, a dark beauty much younger than her husband, sailing down the Halifax in their yacht or waltzing at the Casino. But the day they buried Charles in Pinewood Cemetery was the last day most folks got a look at that mysterious woman. She never again set foot outside the mansion, and few people set foot inside.

Children liked to imagine that her dead husband's ghost kept her locked in a heavily shuttered upper room, but grownups had a story more to their liking. A facelift had gone horribly wrong and left her disfigured for life. Her doctor could swear it wasn't so, but none of his explanations were very satisfying, either.

She moved out in the dead of night in 1941, and soon after the Burgoyne Castle was dismantled. The property, nearly a full city block bounded by Beach Street, Palmetto Avenue, Bay Street, and Volusia Avenue, was now in the hands of William R. Lovett of Jacksonville, the man who founded the Winn-Dixie grocery chain and later bought the Piggly Wiggly grocery chain. The effect of his purchase was to extend the Beach Street business district north of Volusia Avenue—now International Speedway. He named the management company he set up Burgoyne Properties, though no one in the Burgoyne family held any financial interest. Since Lovett's death in 1978, it has been managed by Lovett Family Trusts.

The history of the Burgoyne block since the 1940s is the story of all the ups and downs of Beach Street. By the end of the decade it was home to a Sears & Roebuck, a Furchgott's department store, a Lerners, a Morrison's Cafeteria, the Daytona Theatre, a Krystal, a Walgreens and a grocery store—a Piggly Wiggly, of course.

The area declined quickly in the mid-1970s with the opening of Volusia Mall. The last of the big department stores closed in 1983, leaving Beach Street a virtual ghost town. In 1990, more than 75 percent of the Burgoyne block wa vacant. But in 1991, Burgoyne Properties gambled on redoing building facades. Tenants began returning. Five years later, the block has 100 percent occupancy with interested parties waiting in line for anything that opens. Antiques, a computer store, an art school, cafés, night clubs and a gym have replaced the giant department stores that replaced The Castle. The scale of life has gone from formal dinners in a rich man's Castle to shopping, exercising and casual dining. Burgoyne Properties has found the right fit for a new market and a new generation of Beach Street.

Above: The Burgoyne block of Beach Street circa 1950. The original businesses on the block included a Krystal hamburger restaurant and the Old Daytona Theatre.

Below: The Burgoyne block today. New businesses and modern facades helped bring about a renaissance of Beach Street.

Warner Christian Academy

Above: Warner Christian Academy began in "the Little Red Schoolhouse," the old church chapel which had been painted red.

Below: More than 12,000 students have attended the academy since it opened 25 years ago.

The year was 1932 and Nora Grace Beville was worried about juvenile delinquency. Her husband's family owned the big dairy farms along Beville Road, and their truck drivers were having a bad time with sneaky boys stealing milk tickets—a method used to pay for home delivery in that Depression Era economy. Everything came to a head for Mrs. Beville when she saw a policeman talking to two boys he'd caught in the act. She could hardly imagine anything worse than children in trouble so bad that matters would be taken out of the hands of parents and placed in the hands of legal authorities.

The Bevilles, who made up a large extended family in the area, were followers of the teachings of D. S. Warner, a founding theologian in the Church of God, with its strong emphasis on Christian perfectionism and healing through faith. What Mrs. Beville believed the children of her community needed was a Sunday School where those values could be brought forth.

That Sunday School grew into the White Chapel Church of God, and by 1941, after years of moving from one temporary site to another, the church had its first permanent church building, a small white-framed structure, at the corner of Ridgewood Avenue and Bellewood Road.

Times have changed, and the challenges and temptations facing young people today are far more insidious than Mrs. Beville would ever have imagined in 1932. But one thing that hasn't changed is the White Chapel Church of God's dedication to the youth of Volusia County. And the most visible evidence of that is Warner Christian Academy.

Warner Christian Academy was founded in 1971, the product of longtime pastor Maurice Berquist's desire to expand the congregation's ministry into the community. It was also a time of increasing concern about violence in the area's public schools, leaving many parents looking for an alternative. That first year, the school taught nine first-graders in the original white-frame chapel built in 1941 (now painted red and dubbed "the Little Red Schoolhouse.") For younger children, Warner also had a daycare center. The idea outlined by the first principal, David Black, was to add a new grade each year, but events soon overwhelmed that plan. Another private Christian school closed its doors and parents began calling Warner to ask if there was room for their children. So in 1972, the school opened with grades one through nine and 228 students. A year later there were 440 students. And in the following years, with the school now covering pre-school through high school, more than 12,000 students have attended WCA.

Today, Dr. Russell L. Richards is Headmaster and Reverend Kerry B. Robinson, Senior Pastor of White Chapel, is President. The school is interdenominational, with only about 20 percent of the students coming from White Chapel families. The emphasis is on developing students spiritually, academically, socially, physically, and in service to others. The six general rules of Warner Christian Academy, in place since the school opened, are as follows:

- Education is the primary job of the school.
- The church should always support the school.
- The church should never use the school to convert people from one religion to another.
- The school shall declare itself on the "more conservative" side of every issue.
- Academic quality must be maintained.
- Fees must be kept as low as possible.

The 1996 award-winning Warner Christian Elementary choir performs a musical presentation.

The school is accredited by the Florida Association of Christian Colleges and Schools and is a member of the Association of Christian Schools International. It has hosted the ACSI District Spelling Bee since 1985.

The "Little Red Schoolhouse" is gone today, making way for a physical plant of 198,000 square feet, including large classrooms, two libraries, two gymnasiums, and separate outside playgrounds on a fifteen-acre campus. The libraries have a total of 15,000 volumes. The academic offerings are enhanced by science and computer labs, foreign languages, field trips, music, and an extensive sports program. Each year WCA competes in the Junior Engineering and Technical Society competition.

A number of sports teams compete under the banner of the Warner Christian Academy Eagles, including new teams in swimming and football.

Bible is taught daily and chapel is held once a week. The school promises parents that students are taught in a safe environment by Christian teachers, and all subjects are presented from a Christian perspective.

Perhaps the most telling statistic is that each year, 90 to 100 percent of WCA graduates go on to some form of higher education.

Warner Christian provides a fine education in a Christian environment for students from preschool through high school.

Artesian Pools

Custom designed Artesian Pools create an elegant setting for family gatherings and entertaining.

Artesian Pools of East Florida Inc., one of Central Florida's largest and oldest builders of inground pools has celebrated two decades of service to the Daytona Beach area.

The Company was formed in 1976 by Ben Walters. In 1983 when Walters passed away, the current owner, Roy Lenois, was the vice president and operating manager.

In the beginning, the company operated out of a trailer located at 201 S. Nova Road in Daytona Beach. At that time 201 S. Nova was an open field, and Nova Road had only two lanes, Lenois recalled. As Daytona grew, so did Artesian Pools. Lenois, who grew up in Volusia County, takes particular pride in his company's longevity. In twenty years, Lenois has seen a dozen or more pool companies come and go. "Keeping a company financially sound means good management, fair pricing, good consumer relations, and striving for excellence," says Lenois.

Artesian Pools has continued to grow over the years. Owning its office and construction complex demonstrates its commitment to the community. "It's the duty of every company to remain strong and financially solid," says Lenois. "It's through that commitment that product warranties become important and add value." Artesian Pools boasts a lifetime structural shell warranty which has born the test of over twenty years.

Currently located at 762 S. Nova Road in Daytona Beach, Artesian Pools is staffed by five swimming pool design consultants. They are all trained to help consumers decide which pool best suits their needs and their budget. Each customer receives personalized service and genuine concern for their expectations. Artesian Pools only employs the best subcontractors the industry has to offer in this area and they are closely monitored by the Artesian construction manager. Artesian Pools has constructed pools in the 15 to 100 thousand dollar price range, with the current average being about $18,000. Regardless of price, an Artesian Pool is an investment in your home that you can be proud of. As the slogan says, "We build Fun and We Build it to Last."

Artesian Pool sales people are experts in designing beautiful pools to take full advantage of even the tightest spaces.

Artesian Pools is a full service pool company ready to supply enclosures, decks, and all your pool needs.

Houligan's Irish Sports Pub

Above: Longtime restaurateurs Walter and Tim Curtis built Houligan's into the Halifax area's largest sports bar and restaurant.

The first-class passengers from Daytona Beach had a special request. For their inflight meal, they wanted chicken wings. And not just any wings would do. They had to be *Wally Wings.*

So American Airlines put out the call to Houligan's Irish Sports Pub in Ormond Beach. Order filled, the flight took off with 300 *Wally Wings* and some happy passengers.

Houligan's, the Halifax area's largest sports bar and restaurant and home of the beloved *Wally Wings,* understands how valuable a good wing recipe can be. Thanks to *Wally Wings,* poultry distributors say, Houligan's is distinguished as the largest buyer of chicken wings in all Central Florida.

Located in the South Forty shopping center at 1110 W. Granada Boulevard, Houligan's opened for business just seven years ago. But for Walter Curtis, father of the *Wally Wing,* the restaurant and sports pub represents the culmination of seventeen years of restaurant and nightclub experience in the Halifax area.

The idea for a sports pub came from son Tim Curtis, who joined his father in the restaurant business after college. Tim stumbled onto a similar establishment in Atlanta a decade ago, and the Curtis family immediately recognized that sports-theme bars would be the entertainment of the future.

Over the next few years, the Curtises divested themselves of other restaurants and nightclubs, turning total attention to the creation of Houligan's and the evolution of the sports pub concept.

Today Houligan's boasts 8,000-square-feet of restaurant and bar space, terraced so that every seat has a clear view of several television screens. Altogether, Houligan's has seven ten-foot screens, twenty-five twenty-seven-inch screens, and eight satellite dishes, allowing Houligan's to show every NFL game being broadcast. Not surprisingly, the house stays packed during football season.

The Curtises take particular pride in making Houligan's family friendly. At one time or another, all of the Curtis family—including wife Peggy, daughters Kristen and Lauren, and son Patrick—have worked in the restaurant. The atmosphere is safe and congenial for all age groups.

And the Curtises always make time for civic affairs. Walter and Tim Curtis hold leadership positions with the Chambers of Commerce in Daytona Beach and in Ormond Beach, and serve on local hospital, university, and social service agency boards. Houligan's also sponsors local athletic teams.

But credit the Wally Wings for much of Houligan's success. In Houligan's first year of operation, Wally Wings were the restaurants top seller, even though they weren't yet on the menu. Today, Wally Wings fly out the door at the rate of a million a year.

Poe & Brown

The year was 1943. German submarines lurked just off the coast of Daytona Beach. Nightly blackouts were punctuated by the shrill screams of air raid sirens.

In a panic, Daytona Beach residents Frank and Joan Isaac plunked down $1.30 at the local insurance company for a War Damages Policy. Should their house at 331 S. Ridgewood Avenue, or their 1940 Packard automobile, be bombed during World War II, the Isaacs could rest assured that they were covered for $6,000 in damages.

Today, a framed copy of the Isaac's policy hangs proudly inside the offices of Poe & Brown, Inc. The policy symbolizes a half-century of service to the Daytona Beach/Halifax area. More importantly, the Isaac's policy was the genesis of a corporate journey that would take Poe & Brown from small town local agency to national insurance services powerhouse.

With 1996 revenues of $118 million, Poe & Brown has not only become the largest insurance broker in Florida, it is also the largest in the southeastern United States and twelfth largest in the nation.

Above: J. Hyatt Brown grew his father's small, local insurance agency into the largest agency in the Southeast United States.

Below: Poe & Brown is managed by Charles Lydecker, senior vice president; James Henderson, executive vice president; and Powell Brown, vice president. (Background portrait is of Adrian Brown.)

The company maintains a sales and support staff of 1,050 people nationwide, including about 200 people in Volusia County, making it one of the area's largest employers.

Located at 220 S. Ridgewood Avenue in Daytona Beach, Poe & Brown specializes in insurance for personal and commercial property and casualty accounts, as well as a wide array of employee benefits.

Since 1993, Poe & Brown has been a public company. The biggest stake, however, remains in the hands of the founding Brown family, which owns 23 percent.

The company is headed by J. Hyatt Brown, known throughout Florida for his business and civic involvement. From 1972-1980, Brown represented Daytona Beach in the Florida House of Representatives. While Speaker of the House from 1978-1980, Brown was named one of the fifty "faces of the future" by *Time* magazine. Brown has served in a variety of public and civic areas, including serving on the Florida Board of Regents from 1982-1988. He also serves as trustee and former chairman of the board of trustees of Stetson University.

As chairman, president, and chief executive officer of Poe & Brown, Brown has presided over a thorough transformation of the agency from the small local concern started fifty-seven years ago by his father, the late J. Adrian Brown.

As family legend has it, the Brown insurance agency sprang from his parents' roots in Central Florida. In the 1930s, Adrian Brown, then local manager for the Metropolitan Life Insurance Company, faced transfer to the corporate office in New York. Rather than go, the Browns struck out on their own.

In 1939, when Hyatt was two years old, the Brown & Owen insurance agency opened for business in Daytona Beach. It was a two-man operation—Adrian Brown and his cousin and partner, C. C. Owen—working out of an old building in downtown Daytona Beach on Volusia Avenue (now International Speedway Boulevard).

Like many long-standing family-owned businesses, there are a lot of unusual and interesting stories. During the Brown & Owen years, there was the hurricane of 1949. Sustained winds of 95 miles-per-hour blew the roof off the Riviera Hotel on what is now U.S. 1 in Holly Hill. The pay out was $84,000, a substantial loss in those days. The Brown & Owen Insurance agency was there to make sure all losses were covered, surviving their first major disaster.

By 1955, the eldest Brown son, A. Worley Brown, had graduated from law school and joined his father's insurance agency. In short order, the Browns and cousin Owen parted ways, and the company became Brown & Brown.

J. Hyatt Brown entered the family business in 1959 after graduation from the University of Florida. Change continued at a fast clip. Within two years, his father would retire and his brother would be appointed to head the Florida Industrial Commission, leaving Hyatt back home in charge of the family business.

Hyatt Brown became president of Brown & Brown in 1961. At the time, the company was a small brokerage struggling to become a player in Daytona Beach. Brown employed five people and posted annual revenues of $61,000.

But Hyatt was determined to expand the company. His strategy: target the more profitable big commercial clients and move away from the small personal line policies. Today, commercial clients represent about 90 percent of Poe & Brown's business.

In 1993, Brown & Brown merged with Poe & Associates of Tampa. The firm now has grown to $118 million in revenues. In 1995, *Forbes* ranked Poe & Brown as the thirty-fifth "best small firm in the U.S." With the company's heavy emphasis on attracting high quality, well trained employees, Poe & Brown is well positioned for the next millennium. Its mission statement embodies the Poe & Brown corporate culture: "Poe & Brown is a lean, decentralized, highly competitive, profit oriented sales and service organization comprised of people of the highest integrity and quality, bound together by clearly defined goals and prideful relationships."

Above: Members of the marketing and service departments at Poe & Brown, Inc.

Below: Poe and Brown, Inc., a landmark on Ridgewood Avenue, started in 1939 as a two-man concern and now is one of the Halifax area's largest employers.

Oceans Eleven

Right: Designated a "Hero of the Community," Thomas Staed was selected as an Olympic Torch bearer for his outstanding service to the United Way and to the community.

Below: The Bahama House, Oceans Eleven Resorts' and Daytona Beach's newest hotel, opened in 1992.

Oceans Eleven Resorts Inc., the Halifax area's largest hotel group, was founded by a man who became a national leader in the hotel industry. Tom Staed is presently head of the Florida Commission on Tourism and past president of the American Hotel & Motel Association, Best Western International and the Florida Hotel & Motel Association.

So, few would guess that Oceans Eleven—a group of five oceanfront hotels from Ormond Beach to Daytona Beach Shores—is the product not of a lifelong, carefully executed dream, but rather of a mid-life career change.

The year was 1969. Staed, then thirty-eight, was out of work. He had been a partner in an oil company that had just been sold, and didn't want to return to the practice of law. Most importantly, as a result of the oil company sale, he had some cash that he wished to invest.

At a fall Kiwanis Club meeting, Staed poured out his story to Jack White, a friend and a hotelman fresh from the Beach's golden era. Jack had one piece of advice: ***hotels.***

Throughout his career, Staed has been recognized as a man who thrives on a challenge. True to form, Staed seized White's suggestion and threw himself into the business of innkeeping:

- Late that same year, 1969, Staed bought the 85-room Sanibel Wavecrest with partners White and Daytona Beach lawyer E. William Crotty. Several years later, they sold the hotel for a small profit.
- In 1970, Staed and White bought the 68-room Esquire Hotel, which turned a tidy profit in eighteen months. According to Staed, "The Esquire was a most successful venture and enabled me to simultaneously invest in building several new motel properties.
- In 1972, Staed opened a brand new hotel, the 136-room Silver Beach, which he and his wife, Barbara, helped design.
- Then in 1973 and 1974, Staed and investors, who now sought him out, built eight more hotels and two hotel additions with a total of 1,222 rooms. At its peak, Oceans Eleven owned eleven hotels with 1,500 rooms.

Today, Oceans Eleven operates five hotels totaling 800 rooms, with the Staed family holding controlling interest in four of the properties: the Treasure Island Inn; Bahama House; Beachcomer Oceanfront Inn; and Acapulco Inn.

The Casa del Mar, another Oceans Eleven hotel, is in the process of being converted into a time-share individual ownership joint venture with Avatar Vacation Resorts Inc.

All Oceans Eleven properties cater especially to families, couples, seniors and golfers. The company employs an activities director in each hotel. The week's activities, including supervised play for guests' children, are planned for and adjusted seasonally. For seniors, the hotels sponsor casino nights, and staffers lead guests in water aerobics and on beach walks.

In order to better pursue and service Daytona Beach's increasing golf market, Oceans Eleven has a PGA Pro on staff to work with individuals and groups. An extensive knowledge of area courses, as well as the Oceans Eleven hotels, enables him to custom design golf getaways based on players' budgets and levels of expertise.

In addition to regular hotel operations, Treasure Island Inn also offers a combined 9,000 square feet of meeting space for conventions and other activities, with a professional staff making any type of meeting work well.

All hotels come with the Staed family touch. Although Tom came relatively late to the business, his wife Barbara was twelve when her parents, Evelyn and Monroe Dodd, built their first inn on Daytona Beach. A few years after Tom and Barbara married, Tom got a taste of the business working for his father-in-law before taking the Florida Bar exam and leaving the business for a time practicing law with the largest firm in Daytona Beach.

Barbara has worked for the Oceans Eleven properties since they were founded. She supervises all architectural projects, and oversees all interior design, all landscaping and all furniture, fixture and equipment purchasing. She also is involved in family management decisions.

The Staeds' three daughters, Blaine, Leslie and Whitney, grew up as "hotel kids." Three decades ago, breakfast guests who stumbled into the kitchen of the Aku-Tiki hotel might have seen Leslie seated in a high chair so she could reach the counter, buttering their toast. A few years later, Tom remembers guests questioning why he had an eleven-year-old—once again, Leslie—behind the switchboard.

So taken was Leslie with the hotel business that she worked her way through the dining room, lounge, housekeeping department and front desk at Oceans Eleven before graduating from college with a degree in hotel administration. She then went through the Sheraton's training program before returning to Daytona Beach and the Oceans Eleven operation.

Blaine received a BA from Agnes Scott, and Whitney received a BS in business from the University of Florida and a Master's Degree in business from Florida State University. Blaine and Whitney also worked each summer in an Oceans Eleven hotel, and migrated through many areas of the hotels' various departments.

Today, all three Staed daughters, as well as son-in-law Brian Lansberry, work in the family business. Leslie Staed Bush, former general manager at Bahama House, is now working the operations side of the business. Blaine Staed Lansberry is vice president of marketing, and Whitney Staed is tour and travel sales director. Brian is general manager at Casa del Mar.

With his family behind him, Tom Staed is optimistic about the future of Oceans Eleven and the resort business in the Halifax area. They believe the best days of Volusia tourism are still to come.

Elected in 1996 as vice-chair of the Florida Commission on Tourism, serving under Chairman Lawton Chiles, this is Staed's second tour of duty with the commission (he was the commission's first chairman). As chairman of the new Florida Tourism Industry Marketing Corporation, Staed will be involved with fundraising and for implementing a much larger marketing effort for Florida's public/private tourism corporation. With the new marketing partnership, Staed hopes to put a friendlier face on Florida in the eyes of the world, and envisions significant increases in Florida's tourism.

Below right: Barbara and Tom Staed.

Below left: Whitney Staed (left), Blaine Staed Lansberry (right), and Leslie Staed Bush (front).

Root Organization

Right: Chapman Jay Root created the most recognizable product package in the world: the Coca Cola bottle.

Below: Chapman S. Root and his wife Susan S. Root relocated the family business to Daytona Beach where it grew and prospered.

The year was 1916 and the Coca-Cola Company was trying to solve its biggest problem. In those days, anyone could fill a bottle with brown soda and call it "Coke." What the Atlanta-based soft drink company needed was a distinctive bottle design, instantly recognizable to everyone everywhere. So, they launched a national design contest to find it. Chapman J. Root, owner of the Root Glass Company in Terre Haute, Indiana, decided to enter because the winner also got the right to manufacture the bottle. He assembled a team of glassmakers and began to brainstorm. Someone decided to look up the word "cola" in the encyclopedia, and there on the same page was a picture of a cocoa pod. Its ridged, bowed design, similar to an hour glass, became the inspiration for the most recognizable product package in the world.

Root's glass company, and his interest in various Coca-Cola bottling companies, continued to grow. But the Root family sold the glass company in 1939 to devote itself exclusively to Coca-Cola bottling under the name Associated Coca-Cola Bottling Plants, Inc. The new company would become the nation's largest independent bottler of Coke, dominating the eastern United States with its plants.

In 1950, Chapman S. Root, the twenty-five-year-old grandson of the company's founder, became president of Associated Coca-Cola and relocated the company to Daytona Beach, where he and his partners in the family centralized management of the various bottling plants. But the family's long association with Coca-Cola ended in 1982, in large part due to Chapman S. Root's dismay over the introduction of New Coke. The family sold its interest in the bottling operation back to Coca-Cola for a substantial profit.

The family's timing had always been impeccable. They had devoted themselves solely to Coca-Cola on the eve of World War II, just as American GIs were about to spread the familiar green-glass bottle around the world. They left the business just as another war—the Cola Wars—threatened Coca-Cola's longtime market dominance.

Chapman S. Root diversified his holdings to include communications companies, real estate, even an auto racing team. It seems that whatever caught his interest ended up in his portfolio. At one time he owned a nationally distributed salad dressing, an airline and a fine restaurant, the Pump House East.

His passion for collecting can be seen today in the private museum the family keeps in its company headquarters on Fentress Boulevard. Along with the largest collection of Coca-Cola memorabilia outside of Coca-Cola's own corporate museum are such things as the cradle that rocked John Quincy Adams, headdresses from the movie ***Dances With Wolves***, some 800 teddy bears, and a trout grafted to the head of a bobcat. Behind the headquarters are five antique railroad cars housed in a special train barn. Nearly everything in the museum at one time or another caught the eye of Chapman S. Root or his wife, Susan Spear Root.

Today the company is headed by Chapman Jay Root II, named for his great-grandfather. His background and interests reflect the family's shift

Left: Chapman S. Root was a passionate collector who left the family with the makings of an eclectic museum.

Below: The Root Organization manages its diverse holdings from its Daytona Beach headquarters.

from the midwest to sunny Florida. He races cars and used to own a surf shop. And among his acquisitions are the distribution rights for another Daytona Beach product, Hawaiian Tropic suntan lotion, in the Pacific Rim. He is the eldest of six children and his siblings, Susie, Bill, Chris, John and Preston are all involved in different aspects of the organization and all serve on the board of directors. Family involvement continues as their children enter the business.

The Company manages its diverse portfolio through three divisions. The Operations Division oversees HT International, the Hawaiian Tropic franchise, and Root Communications, which owns television and radio stations. The Real Estate Division manages properties that include the Circle S Ranch in Sublette County, Wyoming, as well as some familiar sites in Daytona beach: the Poe and Brown Office Building; the Coquina Point Subdivision, and the Prudential Securities Office Building. Third is the Financial Portfolio Division for the management of liquid assets.

The Root family has distilled its recipe for success in a mission statement that speaks both for family members and their more than 150 employees. The hallmark of the Root family organization has been and will continue to be self motivation, sensitivity, patience, excellence, creativity, objectivity, determination, and teamwork. It is those qualities that the Root family will take with them into the twenty-first century.

Daytona Beach Community College

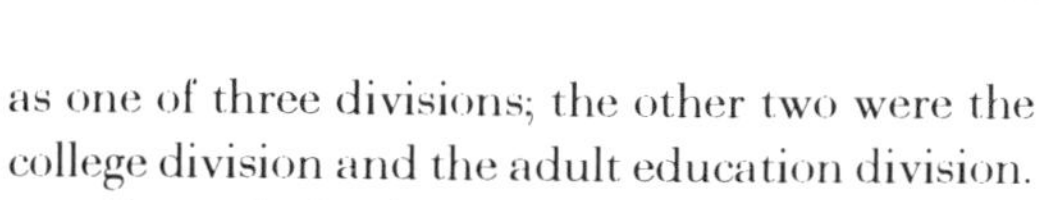

Above: More than 37,000 students attend Daytona Beach Community College each year. Here, students change classes on the Daytona Beach campus.

Below: DBCC is the Halifax area's leading health occupation training facility, providing degree and certificate programs for more than 20 health careers.

The record books will show you that Daytona Beach Community College was founded in 1957, but in reality its history goes back to the tail end of the1929 land boom in Florida. Daytona Beach residents were blissfully unaware of the hard times that would soon come with the Great Depression. The school board opened its new vocational school, optimistically named the Opportunity School.

The school opened in rented rooms atop the Thompson Building on South Beach Street amid high hopes that the great luxury hotels of the day would always keep their doors open and the population would continue its explosive growth, with every new family looking for a home to buy and a car to park in the driveway. But that wasn't to be. As the Depression deepened, the school barely managed to keep its doors open, at one time moving to a small garage on Myrtle Lane with a handful of would-be auto mechanics for students.

In 1937, the school began to regain its footing under its new director, Mary Brennan Karl, who moved it to one of the once swank nightclubs, the Chateau Lido, that was forced by the Depression to close its doors. Mrs. Karl began to fund the school with public subscriptions.

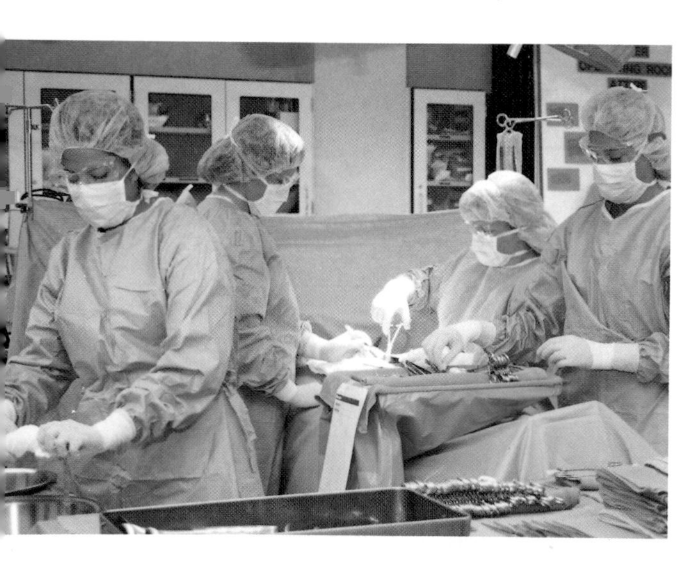

During World War II the school trained hundreds of people for war production work. When the Army closed its convalescent and rehabilitation center in 1946, Mrs. Karl first arranged an interim-use permit, and two years later—the year she died—a restricted deed to the property. The school was renamed the Mary Karl Vocational School; its campus would later become home to Daytona Beach Community College.

In March 1957, Daytona Beach was chosen one of the first six public junior colleges to open in Florida. The Mary Karl school was absorbed as one of three divisions; the other two were the college division and the adult education division.

From the beginning, Daytona Beach Junior College put greater emphasis on job training to meet the needs of local industry, making it much more like the community college of today than the junior college of yesterday, with its purely academic focus. In 1965, DBJC merged with the predominantly African American Volusia County Community College, effectively ending segregation in the Daytona Beach area. In 1971 the school was renamed Daytona Beach Community College.

Today, DBCC has campuses in Daytona Beach, DeBary, DeLand, Flagler/Palm Coast and New Smyrna Beach. More than 40,000 Volusia and Flagler County residents took advantage of DBCC's various academic, cultural, and community offerings last year.

The college has evolved from a small campus into a diverse institution whose mission is multi-faceted. Today, DBCC is the chief provider of work force training for area business and industry. The college has joined in partnership with business - tailoring its occupational training programs to provide students the kind of skills that will make them qualified entry-level employees when they graduate and venture into the region's work force. A host of short-term training programs and other special measures help make education easily accessible to the area's

at-risk and disenfranchised citizens, providing them with critical skills needed to become productive working citizens.

Altogether, some 146 academic and technical programs are offered by the school. The largest share, sixty-four programs, is in the Associate in Arts degree program. The most popular A.A. majors are in business administration, education, engineering, psychology, and computer science. Daytona Beach students pursuing an AA degree can complete the first two years of their baccalaureate degree at DBCC, then transfer to a four-year university, entering at the junior level. By transferring to the University of Central Florida's Daytona Beach campus for their final two years, students can earn their entire bachelor's degree without leaving Daytona Beach.

The school's Technologies Division offers more than 70 programs leading to occupational certificates and Associate of Science degrees. These programs are designed to train students for immediate entry into the work force upon graduation. Ninety-five percent of DBCC's technology graduates get jobs in their field of study.

DBCC's Division of Adult Education and Training has been the fastest growing segment of the college over the past several years. The division provides a variety of adult education programs, including Adult Basic Education, Workplace Literacy, English as a Second Language, Adult Tutoring, General Education Development (GED) and the DBCC Adult High School.

The student population is diverse and reflects the demands for local access to post-secondary education. About 37 percent of students are of traditional college age, 18-24. Another 22 percent are 25-34 years old, 14 percent are 35-44, and 19 percent are 55 or older. More than 100 foreign countries also are represented by DBCC's international student population.

Tomorrow holds the greatest challenges for DBCC. Florida's continued growth is expected to make it the third largest state in the nation by 2000. Locally, Volusia County expects to see a population increase of 26 percent over the next five years, and Flagler County expects 50 percent growth. The institution will continue to aggressively monitor and adapt to the area's work force needs as it plays a critical role in the region's economic development.

Florida's 10 public universities, already offering one of the lowest ratios of universities to population in the country, are not expected to keep pace with the state's growth. This will create an ever increasing demand on DBCC and other community colleges. Many high school graduates who, a decade ago, would have expected to spend four years at a state university, will instead look to spend their first two years of college at DBCC. Because of this projection, the institution also will aggressively monitor and maintain the affordability and quality of its academic programs, which have produced graduates who consistently perform better when they transfer to four-year universities than their counterparts who started at the university as freshmen.

Florida will not only grow more crowded, it will grow more gray, with about a quarter of its residents older than 65 by the turn of the century. It's no surprise then that health and business services will account for almost half the jobs in the service sector, which itself will account for almost 80 percent of all new jobs in Florida over the next decade. And as Florida and the nation move toward a more global economy, international business education and an understanding of cultural diversity are becoming core elements of much of the institution's program curricula.

Above: DBCC's new Bert Fish Building on the west campus in DeLand, including classrooms, a computer laboratory and a state-of-the-art training program in dental hygiene.

Below: Charlene Evans, chair of the applied technology programs.

Ladies Professional Golf Association

Above: The new home of the Ladies Professional Golf Association in Daytona Beach.

Below: LPGA Golfer Laurie Merten shows professional form.

In 1950, the Ladies Professional Golf Association was chartered by a handful of women dedicated to the development of women's professional golf. Now in its fifth decade, the LPGA TOUR and the LPGA Teaching and Club Professional Division are cultivating a worldwide interest in women's golf with fans, sponsors, children, women, golfers, and, more importantly, for charity.

The LPGA TOUR represents the very best in talent and entertainment. The high-profile, multi-million dollar LPGA TOUR continues to attract the world's finest players to test their skills against the best in women's golf. In 1997, the LPGA TOUR will play for approximately $30 million in prize money in over forty tournaments throughout the world. Simultaneously, the LPGA continues to impact the everyday lives of others with dynamic grassroots programs, including executive clinics for business women, the LPGA Urban Youth Golf Program, and the LPGA Girls' Golf Club.

The LPGA Teaching and Club Professional Division has the largest membership of women golf professionals in the country, enjoying unprecedented growth in recent years. These women are teachers, club professionals, coaches, and facility operators. The development and implementation of innovative teaching, educational, and special event programs has established the division as a leader in the golf industry.

But the LPGA is more than golf. The LPGA's commitment to charity has been a well-established tradition with the LPGA tournaments for many years. Approximately seven million dollars is contributed every year from LPGA events, mostly to children's charities. In addition to the charitable activities of the LPGA tournaments, the LPGA established: the LPGA Foundation, a non-profit 501(c)(3) charitable organization; the benefit junior golf; scholarships; the LPGA Hall of Fame; and a catastrophic illness fund. And finally, the LPGA has designated the Susan G. Komen Breast Cancer Foundation as the LPGA's official national charity.

After an extensive search of over 100 prominent communities throughout the United States, the LPGA selected Daytona Beach as the site for its new offices in 1989. The overall plan for the LPGA is to create a first-class destination resort community to showcase the LPGA's National Headquarters and related golf facilities. Designated LPGA INTERNATIONAL, this golf community will feature two eighteen-hole championship courses, a fifty-acre practice facility, the LPGA Golf Academy and Teaching Complex, the LPGA National Headquarters, a 60,000-square-foot luxury clubhouse, residential homes, commercial properties, and a premier resort hotel. LPGA INTERNATIONAL also serves as home to the nationally televised Sprint Titleholders Championship, one of the richest tournaments on the LPGA TOUR.

Together, the LPGA TOUR and the LPGA Teaching and Club Professional Division are leading women's sports towards the LPGA's fiftieth anniversary in the year 2000. As the premier women's sports organization in the world, the LPGA is poised to make the twenty-first century a milestone decade for women in golf.

Daytona International Speedway

Above: The Daytona 500 is stock car racing's premiere event.

From its opening in 1959, the 480-acre Daytona International Speedway has been more than just the home of premiere NASCAR racing events. It's also been a cultural center for Daytona Beach and all of Volusia County. Rarely a week goes by that the Speedway grounds are not used for events that include civic and social gatherings, car shows, athletic games, and production vehicle testing and police motorcycle training. It can also double as a Hollywood soundstage for stock car racing films or television programs.

Without question, though, speed is what it's all about in Daytona, where everyone marks their calendars for the sixteen days of on-track activity dubbed Speedweeks, a varied festival of competition that includes all the stars of stock car racing in the Daytona 500, and drivers from more than twenty nations in the Rolex 24 At Daytona twenty-four-hour sports car race.

Increasingly, the Speedway also has become a destination for tourists wanting to know more about the history of speed in Daytona Beach and its environs. It's a history that includes land speed records on the beach, stock car and motorcycle racing on the same sands, and the complete range of motor sports at the Speedway itself. From NASCAR Winston Cup stock cars roaring by at 190 m.p.h., to AMA Superbikes traveling at 170 m.p.h., to go-karts buzzing along at a startling 125 m.p.h., speed is the name of the game.

DAYTONA USA, which Speedway officials call the "ultimate motorsports attraction" is designed to broaden the entertainment and educational experience for visitors of all ages. The attraction opened in July 1996, and both civic leaders and racing officials hope it will strengthen Daytona's status as an attraction destination.

DAYTONA USA is packed with interactive exhibits, with attention given to both historical perspective and hi-tech thrills.

"We've invested a great deal of thought and creativity to develop an exciting environment that appeals to both the hard-core fans and the most casual observer of the sport," said Lesa Kennedy, executive vice president of the International Speedway Corporation and the driving force behind the venture. "Even if you've never attended a motorsports event or watched one on TV, you can still come away with a truly enjoyable and memorable experience."

Heritage exhibits include Sir Malcolm Campbell's Bluebird V, the car that set the last land speed record on Daytona beach in 1935. At the other end of the technological spectrum is the STP "Daytona Time Trials," where visitors can set up and test drive a stock car through computer simulation.

Below: DAYTONA USA is the latest attraction to open at the Daytona International Speedway. Interactive exhibits can take you back to the days of land speed trials on the beach, or put you behind the wheel of a championship racer via computer simulation.

Peck & Associates Construction Inc.

Top right: A blue neon border atop the Caribbean make this Peck & Associates' condominium a Daytona Beach Shores landmark.

When future historians write the history of the Halifax area, expect to read about the work of Peck & Associates Construction Inc. in a chapter on change and redevelopment in the late 20th century.

As one of the largest — if not the largest — commercial contractors in Volusia County, Peck & Associates has a hand in the way the community looks and feels, and in the way it functions. Several distinctive new commercial and government buildings; the rising skyline along Daytona Beach Shores, which is altering both the scale and ambiance of the beach; and the redevelopment of a significant historic site—the old Ormond Hotel—all are Peck & Associates projects.

But the company is more than a local concern. Peck & Associates has built numerous commercial and industrial projects throughout Florida, including serving as prime contractor on a spin-test facility at the Kennedy Space Center that will be used for testing materials destined for the planned space station.

The luxury Ormond Heritage Condominium (Top Photo) built by Peck & Associates replaced the century-old Ormond Hotel (Right Photo), one of Florida's finest establishments in its day. Rounded edges and interior courtyards retain some of the flavor of the past.

And the company is recognized nationally for the quality of its work. In 1994, Peck & Associates received an award of excellence from the National Commercial Builders Council for construction management of the $40 million expansion of Daytona Beach International Airport. With a joint venture partner, Peck & Associates built the new 166,000-square-foot terminal and customs facility. Not only was this Peck & Associates' biggest job to date, but the airport expansion was the largest construction contract ever awarded by Volusia County.

The airport job helped cement the company's reputation for award-winning work. Peck & Associates, at this writing, has won a total of 81 awards for quality work, including six awards in national competitions and four awards for best work in the Southeast United States. Among the projects honored: the Votran bus transfer station in Daytona Beach, the 23-story Peninsula condominium and the South Daytona City Hall complex.

A recent local award also demonstrates the company's versatility. The Downtown Orlando Partnership gave Peck & Associates the 1995 Golden Brick Award for interior design for the conversion of an old chemical laboratory into a modern recording studio.

Though known for large-scale construction today, Peck started small. In 1974, right out of school, Edwin Peck, Jr. opened for business with $500 capital and little else. Working out of his home, Peck, operating initially as Edwin Peck, Jr. Construction, Inc., took on small jobs— pouring foundations or finishing commercial interiors, renting tools and hiring workers as needed.

His affinity for construction came early. As an 8-year-old in Gainesville, Florida, Peck concocted his first project: a two-story watermelon stand in his front yard. Peck drew the plans and supervised construction. When it was finished, he stored watermelons on the bottom level and kept a lookout for customers from his perch up top. The watermelons sold for 25-cents a piece and paid for the stand.

Every summer, the Pecks and two or three other Gainesville families vacationed together at

Daytona Beach. After several years, Peck's parents, Hilda and Edwin Peck, Sr., came up with the idea of creating a permanent vacation home. The idea caught fire and spread. Pretty soon, the senior Peck was developing the first oceanfront condominium in Daytona Beach Shores, the 60-unit Surfside Club.

Edwin Peck, Jr. eventually made Daytona Beach his home. Nine years after starting his business, and with interest rates rising, the construction industry began to change. Jobs began to fall into two categories: big, multi-million dollar developments and small remodeling projects. Peck made the leap into major contracting in 1983 by selling stock to raise capital. The move was so successful that, within three years, Peck was able to repurchase all outstanding stock from his investors.

Today, Peck & Associates constructs restaurants, churches, offices, manufacturing facilities, schools and other commercial and industrial buildings throughout the state. Some of the company's more well known clients include Wal-Mart, Hawaiian Tropic, Garden Ridge, Walgreens and Digital Computer as well as Daytona Beach Community College, Halifax Medical Center and the News-Journal.

Peck & Associates is well known to the general public for building a string of high-rise condominiums, including the Caribbean and the Peninsula, one of the area's tallest, which helped change the skyline in Daytona Beach Shores.

As contractor on the new $23 million Ormond Heritage Condominium which replaced the historic Ormond Hotel in Ormond Beach, Peck worked with the architect to give the new condominium buildings some flavor of the past. Walkways connecting the three condominium buildings, rounded edges on the buildings, interior courtyards and pagodas all are echoes of the old Ormond Hotel.

Peck gives credit for Peck & Associates' success to employees selected for their expertise and commitment to quality. As his company's motto says, "Attention to detail, understanding of time restrictions, quality within budget and the drive for perfection are characteristics you'll find in the people of Peck & Associates."

Halifax Medical Center is one of Peck & Associates' many commercial clients. Here, the hospital's newest Peck-constructed wing.

The laboratory building on the south campus of Daytona Beach Community College is one of many school buildings constructed by Peck & Associates.

The terminal at Daytona Beach International Airport is an award-winner for Peck & Associates. Peck served as construction manager for the $40 million airport expansion.

Interior design is one of Peck & Associates' specialties. Brithaus Recording Studio in Orlando offers customers a relaxed atmosphere.

Halifax Fish Community Health

Halifax Hospital Medical Center *Board of Commissioners*

James H. Foster

Marilyn W. Coble

Sylvester Covington

Peromnia Grant

Robert C. Elston

Edwin W. Peck

Mary Jo Stansfield

Ron R. Rees
President/CEO
Halifax Community
Health System

Southeast Volusia Hospital District
Board of Commissioners

Aubrey S. Lunsford

John M. Albright

Richard Bailey

Frances R. Ford

Arden W. Kelley

John S. Massey

Rev. Donald L. Shobert

James R. Foster
President/CEO
Bert Fish Medical
Center

As this book clearly depicts, each new wave of challenge that has washed across Daytona Beach, has been met by far-sighted leaders, ready to respond.

In the fall of 1996, the latest of those leaders stood to be counted in the arena of Healthcare. The commissioners of the Halifax Hospital Medical Center and the Southeast Volusia Hospital District joined forces to create a healthcare system for the 21st Century—Halifax Fish Community Health.

The Halifax Commissioners set policy for Halifax Medical Center and affiliated organizations including Florida Health Care Plans, a hospice program, home health agency, nursing home, other insurance interests, a physician-hospice organization and a community health agency. The Southeast Volusia Board establish policies that guide Bert Fish Medical Center, southeast Volusia clinics, a physician organization and other healthcare services. Both boards, appointed by the Governor, are charged with levying property taxes sufficient to assure the provision of care for those in their service areas, uninsured and unable to pay for care.

The two boards, knowing that managed care has mandated mergers in many areas, and puts a premium on regional service, determined that they could set a new pattern for partnership that would assure their communities of continued representation and the determination of how local taxes would be levied and local services offered. In a series of meetings involving representatives of their medical staffs, they crafted an inter-local agreement through which a new system was created to provide the economies and efficiencies of centralized management, but retain the determination of service levels, budgets and indigent care in each community.

The product of that partnership, Halifax Fish Community Health, came into being October 1, 1996. It was voted into being and will be led in its developmental stages by the community leaders shown on this page. They are as diverse as the communities they represent, and as determined as any in the healthcare field to see that the needs of those communities are met with quality care, respect for individuals, and wise use of tax dollars entrusted to their use.

Halifax Medical Center and Bert Fish Medical Center and their affiliated companies will continue to have a strong identity in Daytona Beach and New Smyrna Beach. Through Halifax Fish Community Health, that identity will be supported with good medicine delivered by quality people working in an environment that makes the most of change.

Halifax Medical Center

Halifax Medical Center, Daytona Beach

In 1926, the Florida Legislature created the Halifax District Hospital and authorized the Governor to appoint a Board of Commissioners to see that medical care was made available to all residents, regardless of their ability to pay.

In 1996, Commissioners appointed by the Governor continue that mission, setting policy for a facility that has grown from 125 beds when it opened in 1928, to the cornerstone of a healthcare system that reaches out into the communities it serves with a wide range of services tailored to the needs of area residents. Halifax Medical Center is a full-service medical institution with 495 licensed beds. Its main campus is supplemented by branch "hospitals without beds" meeting a wide range of outpatient needs in Port Orange and Ormond Beach.

The Kerman Regional Oncology Center, a part of Halifax Medical Center is one of the largest community outpatient cancer treatment facilities in the Southeast. Its nationally-affiliated oncologists regularly participate in national clinical trials assuring its patients of home-town access to the latest treatment techniques. Halifax Medical Center is the only area hospital to provide a specialized pediatrics unit and neonatal unit, to provide adolescent behavioral services, and offers the only Level III trauma center on Florida's Funcoast. A fitness center, extensive pastoral care program, family practice residency program and radiologic technology and radiation therapy schools, coupled with clinical affiliations with Daytona Beach Community College, University of Central Florida, Bethune Cookman College and others, underscore the commitment of policy-makers and operational personnel alike to "people-centered" programs and service within the community.

That service is furthered through the operation of community-centered clinics throughout its service area and outreach programs that give meaning to the determination of its personnel that its initials—HMC—truly stands for Halifax Means Caring.

Halifax Medical Center, Ormond Beach

Halifax Medical Center, Port Orange

Holly Hill

Florida Health Care Plans

Daytona Beach

The waves of challenge depicted on these pages have been fully shared by Florida Health Care Plans, the region's only locally-based health maintenance organization. It is a success story built on the achievements of Daytona Beach area residents as knowledgeable consumers and skilled providers of quality health care.

Florida Health Care Plans began operations on July 1, 1974, on the cutting edge of changes in the delivery of health care that have become commonplace today. In 1979, it was the second health maintenance organization, or HMO, in the United States to receive accreditation from the Joint Commission on Accreditation of Healthcare Organizations (JCAHO), which is regarded as a standard of the industry. In 1991, and at each renewal since, JCAHO has reaccredited Florida Health Care Plans "With Commendation," the highest level of industry recognition. Florida Health Care Plans was initially designated by the Agency for Health Care Administration as an Accountable Health Partnership in 1994, a designation that continues.

But the real story of Florida Health Care Plans is in its service to the community. By keeping its focus on a confined area of Florida's Funcoast and through its affiliation with what has become Halifax Fish Community Health, the organization has been able to put local needs and services first. If a member has a question or a problem to be answered or resolved, the president of the company has an open office door in the heart of the area and a number listed in the phone book!

Service to employers in providing comprehensive group coverage, care tailored to the needs of the Medicare population, and community-based facilities supplemented by the most extensive network of contract physicians and services of any health maintenance organization serving the area are the reasons that Florida Health Care Plans is more than a business—it's a good neighbor.

Orange City

New Smyrna Beach

Embry-Riddle Aeronautical University

Above: An aerial view of the Embry-Riddle Aeronautical University campus in Daytona Beach, Florida.

Embry-Riddle Aeronautical University began in the age of barnstorming daredevils and their looping, rolling bi-planes—the 1920s. John Paul Riddle made his living as a barnstormer, flying town to town, offering flying lessons to the strong-hearted. But Riddle, who with his friend, student, and financier, the wealthy young T. Higbee Embry, started the Embry-Riddle Company, was among a handful of aviation pioneers who realized the future of commercial aviation depended on safety and reliability, not seat-of-the-pants heroics.

Riddle and Embry went into business selling airplanes in 1925. The next year they added a flight school and air-mail contracts to their portfolio. Soon, there were plenty of other flying schools, and the poor instruction they offered resulted in most of the era's aviation deaths. Embry-Riddle, on the other hand, produced pilots, not simply people who knew how to fly. Most people can learn to fly in a day, but Embry-Riddle produced reliable professionals with two-years of study and training under their belts.

In 1929, the Embry-Riddle Company became part of the corporation that would later become AVCO, and plans were laid for what would be the nation's first aviation university. That initial effort ended in failure, due in part to the Depression, but also to the proliferation of cheaper, less thorough flying schools. By 1930, both Embry and Riddle had sold their common stock to another AVCO subsidiary, American Airlines, and the nation's oldest flying school was closed.

But the Embry-Riddle story was far from over. Higbee Embry moved to California, where he died in 1946. But Paul Riddle headed to Miami, and revived the school under the name Embry-Riddle School of Aviation. By the start of World War II, Embry-Riddle stood ready to train 26,000 British and American pilots, mechanics, and technicians over the course of the war.

Riddle sold his interest in 1944. By the mid-1960s the school, now the Embry-Riddle Aeronautical Institute, was under the leadership of Jack Hunt, a former Navy blimp pilot who had piloted his blimp around the world on the longest sustained and un-refueled flight ever made. But soon after Hunt took over, the Dade County Port Authority decided to drive Embry-Riddle out of Miami by closing the Tamiami Airport. The school decided to relocate rather than shut its doors, and began to search for a new home.

Daytona Beach, with lots of open air space and a hunger for growth, was the natural selection. To help the school relocate, the local Jaycees and the Committee of 100 raised much of the money required for the move. In 1965, the school began operation at its new home, the Daytona Beach Municipal Airport.

In 1970, the Embry-Riddle Aeronautical Institute became Embry-Riddle Aeronautical University, and the change in status sparked the school's greatest era of growth and expansion. Today, with residential campuses in Daytona Beach and Prescott, Arizona, Embry-Riddle is accredited by the Commission on Colleges of the Southern Association of Colleges and Schools and offers its more than 20,000 students courses leading to associate's, bachelor's and master's degrees suitable for a career in aeronautical science, computer science, engineering, management and technology as well as numerous FAA-approved certification courses.

Under the leadership since 1991 of Dr. Steven Sliwa, the university has added six new campus buildings, and reached out to students worldwide through its Extended Campus which includes a network of more than 100 off-campus education centers in the United States and Europe.

Below: Opportunities for research can include designing systems like this one-of-a-kind passenger jet simulator. Engineering, computer science, and flight students started with a Boeing 707 simulator, changed all the internal hardware, linked it with state-of-the-art video animation computers, and produced a simulator that can be programmed to emulate the characteristics of any airliner currently on the market.

Palm Plaza

Above: The late Larry Fornari Sr. and wife, Marie Grace, built the Palm Plaza into one of Daytona Beach Shores' premier hotel resorts.

Below: The Palm Plaza offers guests a stunning view of the Atlantic Ocean.

At the end of Simpson Street in Daytona Beach Shores, a little ocean-front park with flowering cactuses and a wooden deck overlook offers a tiny respite from the bustle of the beach. Fittingly, the park is dedicated to the late Larry Fornari, Sr., owner of the Palm Plaza resort hotel who is memorialized in a plaque as "a tireless servant to the community."

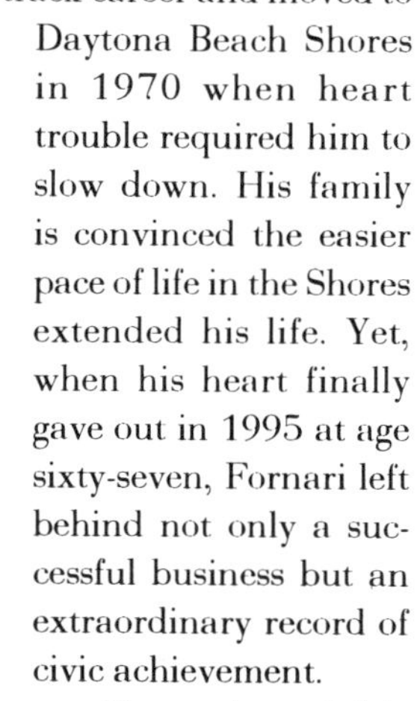

Fornari left a fast-track career and moved to Daytona Beach Shores in 1970 when heart trouble required him to slow down. His family is convinced the easier pace of life in the Shores extended his life. Yet, when his heart finally gave out in 1995 at age sixty-seven, Fornari left behind not only a successful business but an extraordinary record of civic achievement.

Fornari and his wife, Marie Grace, had vacationed in Daytona Beach Shores. But that was the limit of their experience with beach resort hotels when they packed up their three small children in Indianapolis, bought the twenty-room Mermaid Beach Motel and moved the family into an apartment over the office.

The Fornaris worked tirelessly as a team to build their business. With just a few employees to help, they spent five years working together without a vacation. Fornari handled all the business and financial aspects of the business while Grace handled all the housekeeping functions and other daily duties.

Meanwhile, Fornari indulged his love for politics, serving as mayor of Daytona Beach Shores, president of the Daytona Beach Shores Chamber of Commerce, and twice as president of the Daytona area hotel and motel association. In 1975 and again in 1992, Fornari was honored by the chamber as "Citizen of the Year." He is credited with organizing voters in the late 1970s to stop Daytona Beach from annexing the Shores, and with leading a fundraising effort to pay for city beautification.

Over the years, the Fornaris invested in numerous hotels and condominiums, culminating in 1989 with the Palm Plaza, a ninety-eight-room high rise at 3301 South Atlantic Avenue. Grace Fornari personally handled all the design and interior decorating for the new building, duties she still performs.

In recent years, the Fornaris' son, Larry, assumed responsibility for the family business and has jumped into civic life, following closely in his father's footsteps.

Barnett Bank

Above: The Barnett Bank clock, a landmark in DeLand, has graced the front of the bank building since Barnett came to town in 1929. The clock was refurbished in 1985.

Below: Barnett Bank's customers now are located throughout the Halifax Area and are served by 30 offices such as this at 1025 International Speedway Boulevard.

Look up "everywhere" in a dictionary and you're likely to find the familiar green and white logo of Barnett Bank. In fact, it's hard to imagine a time when the Barnett name evoked a family and not an institution, but more than a century ago, Barnett was not a bank at all but a man named William Barnett, a transplanted Kansan who parlayed his $43,000 life savings into a sturdy enterprise he called the Bank of Jacksonville.

Barnett was still a family business when it came to Volusia County during the Great Depression, and the bank was still many years away from becoming the largest and wealthiest in Florida.

In 1929, the First National Bank in DeLand, like thousands of other banks, failed. But just up the road in Jacksonville, the Barnett family's bank survived. It was a bank that had a good deal of practice surviving. Since William Barnett had opened for business in 1877, the bank had weathered two yellow fever epidemics, a typhoid epidemic, and a devastating freeze that bankrupted hundreds of other businesses in East Florida. Even a fire that destroyed most of Jacksonville left the Barnett building unscathed.

A delegation of businessmen from DeLand's Chamber of Commerce was dispatched to Jacksonville to make a personal appeal to Bion Barnett, son of founder William, to expand his operation into Volusia County. Convinced that there was opportunity in DeLand, the Barnetts formed a bank holding company to acquire and re-open failed banks, including what they named the Barnett National Bank of DeLand.

Today, Barnett Bank is in 234 cities in Florida and Georgia. One of every four dollars deposited in a Florida bank goes into one of Barnett Bank's 596 offices. But the Barnett office in DeLand, headquarters for Barnett Bank in Volusia and Flagler counties, holds the distinction of being just the third bank in the Barnett family tree. Bill Barnett, grandson of the founder, was the long-time chairman in Volusia County until his retirement, and chairman emeritus until his recent death.

Barnett does business with more households—78,000—in Volusia and Flagler counties than any other financial institution, and maintains a strong presence in the Halifax area. Barnett, chosen by many customers for convenience and service quality, has thirty locations in the two counties, and employs some 450 people.

The company continues to expand in product areas such as investment management and insurance, and recently announced an agreement with Publix Supermarkets to locate branches in Publix stores.

And the company continues the Barnett family's commitment to the community. In 1888, when nearly 500 citizens of Jacksonville were killed by yellow fever, the Barnetts suspended all payments on installment loans as a relief measure. A hundred years later in Volusia County, Barnett gave Stetson University its largest corporate gift ever: the $400,000 Barnett scholarship fund which helps several students every year further their education.

Hudson Tool and Die

Above: Hudson Tool & Die Co., Inc., as it appeared in 1968 when the plant first opened for business in Ormond Beach.

Below: Hudson Tool & Die Co., Inc., today. The workforce has increased by a factor of six since the early days in Ormond Beach. The company now employes about 275 people.

Hudson Tool and Die of Ormond Beach is a company close to the hearts of many cardiac patients.

Three decades ago, experiments with implantable heart pacemakers failed when bodily fluids corroded the pacemakers' epoxy casings. Then Hudson Tool and Die crafted the first tiny stainless steel shells to protect the lifesaving works.

Today, Hudson remains a major supplier of implantable heart pacemaker cases, now drawn in titanium metal, and pacemaker batteries. And the company's reputation for ingenuity and precision work when precision counts has spread worldwide.

Located on a twelve-acre campus at 1327 North U.S. 1, Hudson is one of the largest manufacturers in Volusia County.

The plant produces a wide variety of special metal parts for customers from forty-nine states and fifteen countries. And with Hudson parts aboard the old moon rovers left behind by Apollo astronauts, the company can even boast of being an official tool and die supplier to the moon.

With annual revenue of over $20 million, Hudson is a mid-size company. But in Hudson's niche of precision, deep-drawn, metal enclosures, few companies in the world can match Hudson's size or performance.

The result, as President Paul Clare notes, is some pretty interesting business:

Each space shuttle contains more than 120 Hudson-made parts.

Sensors in the first mass-produced airbags for Chrysler were encased in Hudson parts.

And the main body of Hewlitt Packard's Atomic Clock was created by Hudson, winning the company the runner-up award in the 1996 Precision Metalforming Association design competition.

In all, Hudson has designed and custom-built tooling to stamp out more than 20,000 different parts for specialized jobs worldwide.

But Hudson also has a library of more than 9,000 standard round and rectangular parts produced regularly for its more than 1,500 customers.

Hudson was founded in 1940, when a Czechoslovakian toolmaker named Charles Batka immigrated to the United States and opened shop in Hudson County, New Jersey. Early on, Hudson developed its reputation for precision, deep-drawn work. So much so that by the 1950s, Hudson's specifications were used as the basis for U.S. Military quality standards.

The impetus for Hudson's eventual migration to Florida was a 1958 ad in the ***Wall Street Journal*** offering industrial acreage in Ormond Beach. Much to the consternation of city leaders trying to boost business, Batka bought up all seventy acres, then sat on it for nearly a decade. He finally opened a second plant there in 1968.

In 1984, five years after Batka's death, his son sold the company to JSJ Corporation, a private holding company from Grand Haven, Michigan, which then hired Clare as president. Clare, along with vice presidents Ray Michaels and Pete DiLella, consolidated Hudson's headquarters and all manufacturing operations at its 110,000 square-foot Ormond Beach plant in 1991.

Today, Hudson employs 275 people, from press operators to design engineers, to whom Clare gives credit for the company's continuing success. Their cumulative knowledge and dedication to success, Clare says, enables Hudson to meet new challenges and maintain the high standards for which the company has long been respected around the world.

Memorial Health Systems

Memorial Health Systems has a single goal: promoting good health.

That's why for three decades, the three hospitals that make up Memorial Health Systems have been providing high-quality health care and sophisticated technology to the residents of Volusia and Flagler Counties.

The hospitals are community-owned and organized on a not-for-profit basis.

Memorial Hospital-Ormond Beach

Since opening its doors in 1967, Memorial Hospital-Ormond Beach has become well-known for providing outstanding and cost-effective medical/surgical services to area residents.

This 205-bed, acute-care facility offers more than 300 physicians. Key services include: the Memorial Heart Institute, with Volusia and Flagler counties' only open heart surgery program; the Memorial Cancer Care Center, providing radiation therapy and medical oncology; the BirthCare Center, offering private suites and family-centered birth care; home health care; and a transitional care unit.

Memorial Hospital-Flagler

Memorial Hospital-Flagler extends the tradition of excellence in patient care to the residents of Palm Coast and Flagler County. This eighty-one-bed facility, acquired by Memorial Health Systems in 1989, provides high-quality medical care and medical/surgical services. It has a growing medical staff of more than eighty physicians. Among the many services offered by Memorial Hospital-Flagler are: home health care; hospice care; respite care; and a transitional care unit.

In late 1993, Memorial Health Systems purchased 101 acres on the northwest corner of State Road 100 and Interstate 95 for the future development of a health care/hospital campus to meet the long-term needs of Flagler County.

Memorial Hospital-West Volusia

The newest member of Memorial Health Systems, Memorial Hospital-West Volusia, offers a full spectrum of quality medical and surgical services to the residents of DeLand and western Volusia County. The 156-bed hospital opened in 1962 and joined the Memorial Health Systems family of hospitals in 1994. It has more than 130 physicians on its medical staff and includes these special services: a BirthCare Center; a Sleep Disorders Center; the West Volusia Breast Center; and home health care.

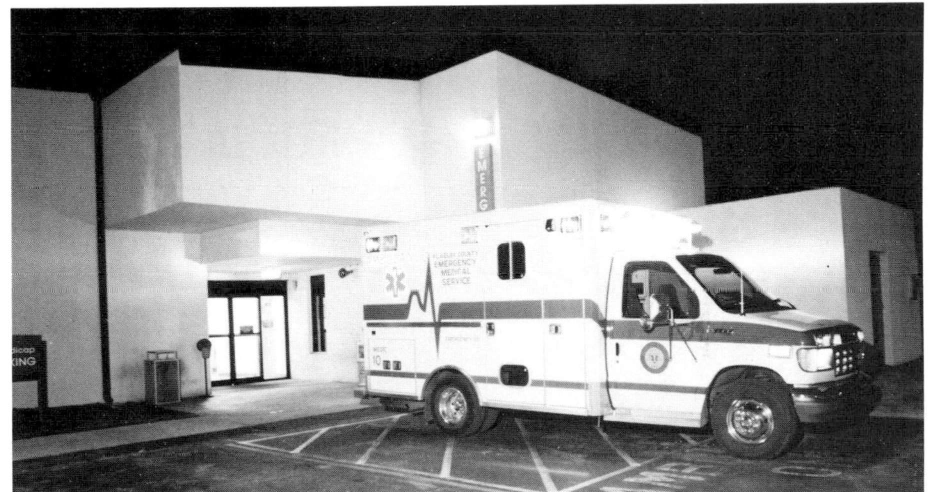

Hawaiian Tropic

Above: *The first batches of Hawaiian Tropic suntan oil were brewed by Ron Rice in this garbage can. Eight years later, Rice opened his first plant in Ormond Beach.*

Below: *Rice's proudest achievement is 6-year-old daughter Sterling, who will inherit the suntan lotion empire one day.*

In 1965, Ron Rice was an underpaid high school chemistry teacher and part-time lifeguard. On weekends and after school, he'd wheel his salt-eaten Mustang along the beach, loaded to the windows with bottles of homemade suntan oil, hoping to make enough extra cash that he could afford hamburgers for dinner instead of canned vegetable beef soup.

An empire in the making? No one would have thought so, least of all Rice. But today he is sole owner of the world's second-largest producer of suntan products. Sales of Hawaiian Tropic products top $200 million a year, and his personal net worth is in the neighborhood of $100 million. And, lest we forget, his Hawaiian Tropic Girls have joined the Dallas Cowboy Cheerleaders and the Swedish Bikini Team in the pantheon of pop icon pulchritude.

Rice still sees himself as a country boy from the hills of North Carolina, someone who hasn't forgotten his friends—in fact, he's made some of his old lifeguard buddies millionaires—or his roots—his daughter will attend public schools; he sees himself as an example of the potential in every public school teacher.

But in the beginning, his teacher's salary and his part-time incomes as a football coach and lifeguard were bringing in just $4,300 a year. Sitting on his lifeguard tower on long summer days, Rice would survey the scene around him, the bathers and all their beach paraphernalia, trying to think up some way to bring in some extra cash.

Back in the early 1960s, Sea & Ski, then one of the top selling suntan lotions, had little competition, no marketing and no pizzazz. In short, nothing to inspire brand loyalty.

Rice himself had fair, hard-to-tan skin. So, naturally, on a trip to Hawaii he had been particularly impressed by the natives' rich chocolate skin and luxuriant hair, and wondered if the coconut oil he saw them rubbing into their skin and hair would work for everyone.

Starting with $500 borrowed from his father and a limited knowledge of chemistry, Rice in 1965 began experimenting, mixing up brews of natural tropical ingredients in a $4 metal garbage can in his garage. The first batch, if it didn't produce a superior suntan, was at least edible: a concoction of coconut oil, avocados, bananas, nuts, and flowers.

That summer while on lifeguard duty, Rice used tourists as guinea pigs, slathering one arm with one experiment, the other arm with another experiment and waiting to see which side tanned best and appealed most. Soon, Hawaiian Tropic—originally called Tropic Tan until Rice discovered he was violating someone else's trademark—was in production.

Rice's first bottle filling machine employed the gravity method and two eleven-year-old kids who held glass bottles at the end of a hose stuck in the bottom of the garbage can. The little factory produced six hundred bottles a day. Rice would load up the Mustang and ride down the beach, distributing his product to the motel pool decks and lifeguard stands.

"The crazy part about it was when it got started I couldn't keep up with demand," Rice recalls.

No one had ever seen a suntan oil like Hawaiian Tropic, with its rich, natural ingredients and the wonderful fragrance of banana and coconut. It didn't hurt either that the lifeguards, virtual tanning gods to the minds of pale-faced tourists, were talking it up around the pool decks

Left: Rice poses with 1996 winners of the Miss Hawaiian Tropic International pageant which was started by Rice (who doesn't believe in normal advertising) as a promotional event.

Below right: Hawaiian Tropic models go to France to support one of the Hawaiian Tropic race cars at 24 Hours at LeMans.

Below left: Hawaiian Tropic girls give one of Ron's friends, the late, great, Benny Hill, bright red smacks on the cheeks.

and the beach. The lifeguards, of course, were Rice's friends, working on commission.

Hawaiian Tropic quickly developed a cult-like following thanks in large part to Rice's inability to satisfy the demand. As fast as Rice could restock a beach concessionaire from the back of his Mustang, some northerner would come along and buy up the whole display for resale back home.

In 1973—four years after Hawaiian Tropic was born—Rice says he knew he had a tiger by the tail, and that he would have to expand the business or lose it. That year, he quit teaching, got a small bank loan, and built a small plant. Although the plant enabled Rice to increase production, it still wasn't enough: distributors would line up at the plant with blank checks made out to Rice ready to load up as much oil as he could make.

Today, Hawaiian Tropic's headquarters and factory in Ormond Beach cover more than 240,000 square feet, and Rice makes more than 700 skin care products using over 1000 ingredients. The plant runs twenty-four hours a day, fifty-one weeks a year, producing up to 50 million packages a year.

Rice, who in the 1960s anticipated the movement toward natural products with his early suntan oils, has in more recent years led the industry in improving and strengthening sunblocks. Hawaiian Tropic was the first company in the United States to mass market suntan lotions with an SPF rating higher than 15. Protective lotions now dominate the business.

With Rice's fortune has come fame and famous friends, who crowd his parties and mingle with the bathing beauties at his annual Hawaiian Tropic pageants. But in the living room of his $5.5 million beachfront home sits the garbage can in which he mixed his first batch of Hawaiian Tropic. Now silverplated, it's the ultimate reminder of how far this country boy has come.

SunTrust

Right: Convenience has always been a hallmark of SunTrust Banks. Here, the old Commercial Bank, which later became SunTrust, was located on Volusia Avenue in the downtown business district.

Below: The latest convenience in banking is SunTrust's new mobile automatic teller machine which can be set up in minutes at festivals or any place people gather.

Long before automatic teller machines introduced the world to the convenience of walk-up banking, there was L. A. "Pop" Coleman.

Throwing open the window of his front corner office at the Industrial Savings Bank, Coleman, a jack-of-all-trades who founded the bank in 1936, spent his days chatting up passersby on the sidewalk along Volusia Avenue.

And if someone happened by who needed a loan for, maybe, a washing machine or a refrigerator, all the better. Coleman would write up the paperwork and pass the cash through the window.

In those days, when banking was a handshake deal, a bank officer asking a customer for collateral was set straight by "Pop" calling across the room, "Give the boy the money and just get him to sign his name."

Bankers today run a much tighter ship. But SunTrust, the successor to the old Industrial Savings Bank and one of the three largest banking companies in Volusia County, still builds business by building personal relationships with its customers.

In six decades, the bank that Coleman founded has gone through four name changes and two major ownership changes to become a member of the SunTrust family.

Industrial Savings Banks were only one step up from a finance company, making small loans for such things as household appliances. So in 1946, the bank's charter was changed and the bank renamed Commercial Bank to do business with commercial establishments. That same year, "Pop" Coleman turned the bank over to his son, Henry Coleman, Sr.

One of the younger Coleman's proudest achievements was creating the first drive-up window in the Halifax area—and perhaps in the entire state. As his son, Hank, Jr., recalls, Coleman sheered off a back corner of the bank building to enable cars to pull up close to the teller.

Hank, Jr. was elevated to the office of president one year after the family sold its interest in the bank to First at Orlando (later SunBank), then one of about eighteen holding companies in the country authorized to buy and own banks.

The Colemans became the largest shareholders in the holding company and retained control over the Daytona bank's management.

Over the years, banks in Georgia, Tennessee and Alabama joined SunBank as part of SunTrust. In the fall of 1995, all of the banks adopted the name SunTrust.

Today SunTrust maintains twenty-four branches in Volusia and Flagler Counties with deposits of $1 billion in the two-county area.

The Martin Companies

The less noticed about The Martin Companies' work the better. If the plumbing flushes, if the flooding recedes, if the highway is smooth—in short, if life is free of those aggravating bumps and backups—then Martin has done its job.

That's because Martin builds the infrastructure—the roads, utilities, and the drainage systems—that makes a community work.

Martin, with headquarters at 1801 S. Nova Road in South Daytona, is one of the 200 largest privately held companies in Florida. Headed by two brothers, Robert and Richard Martin, both Daytona Beach natives, the organization includes Volusia County's oldest road paving firm, Martin Paving Company, founded by the brothers' father.

In 1955, Mac Martin and a partner who lasted less than a year went into business under the name L & M Paving & Construction Company. They started with a handful of employees and equipment worth $2,000—an old dump truck and a farm tractor with a scraper. For years the company operated out of Martin's home, surviving primarily on the construction of parking lots for the new hotels going up on the beachfront. Martin added a brick distributorship in 1965 called Martin Brick, now the largest in Central Florida.

When the Martin brothers took over from their father in 1978, the companies employed a dozen people and averaged $500,000 in annual sales. Since then, the Martins took on partners in several new ventures and dramatic growth has brought the company to 300 employees, a 600-vehicle fleet, and $50 million in yearly sales. The Martins built on their strength in infrastructure with two of the new companies: Scott-Martin Construction Company, an underground utilities contractor which was sold in 1996, and Ward-Martin Concrete Company, which builds curbs and sidewalks.

But a third partnership took the Martins into a new and high-profile arena. In a public-private venture with the city of Daytona Beach, Martin-McGrath Company developed the oceanfront hotel which quickly became one of the area's most recognizable landmarks. Now the Adam's Mark Daytona Beach Resort, the hotel was part of a city plan to redevelop the Main Street area.

Today, the Martins are winding down their development partnership and refocusing the companies on major highway and airfield construction.

Above: The Martin Companies is headed by brothers Robert D. Martin, chairman and chief executive officer (right), and Richard K. Martin, president.

Below: The Martin Companies is one of the leading highway and heavy construction contractors in the Halifax area and Central Florida.

University of Central Florida

Above: The newest building on the University of Central Florida's Daytona Beach campus, opened in 1990, has an auditorium, classrooms, seminar rooms, and faculty suites.

The University of Central Florida was an idea born in 1963, the heyday of America's space program, when the nation's commitment to land a man on the moon was bringing the world to Cape Canaveral and Central Florida. But like many big ideas, it had to start small. Long before classes ever began, Florida Technological University (as it was first known) was housed above a drugstore in downtown Orlando.

When Dr. Charles Millican, the school's first president, drove out Route 426 to find his undeveloped campus in eastern Orange County, he had to ask directions from a gas station attendant. As it turned out, the directions were wrong and Millican missed by about five miles.

A public university in Central Florida had long been the goal of the area's business community, but it was the arrival of NASA and contractors like Martin Marietta that assured their success. By the time the first 2,000 students began classes in the fall term of 1968, the school was already beginning to outgrow its technological university status. Plans for Disney World, EPCOT, and other tourist attractions would soon make Central Florida one of the fastest growing areas of the country, and the university was ready with programs in business administration and education. Fifty-five bachelor's degrees were offered by five colleges within the university. The next year, seventeen masters programs were added, and in 1980, the first Ph.D. program was offered.

Center: Volusia County students can have the experience of a four-year college without ever leaving home by completing their associate degrees at Daytona Beach Community College, then proceding with their bachelor's degrees at the University of Central Florida.

Today, UCF's enrollment tops 28,000. It has a faculty of 700 and 150 degree programs. In addition to its main campus and the Daytona Beach campus, UCF has a third campus in Cocoa and centers in downtown Orlando and south Orlando.

Because the Daytona campus is located adjacent to Daytona Beach Community College, students are able to make a seamless transition from the first two years of undergraduate study at DBCC to the upper division programs at UCF.

Since the school's first semester of operation in 1968, Volusia and Flagler Counties have been served by UCF's Daytona Beach campus. With student enrollment increasing about 15 percent each year, the Daytona Beach campus is one of the fastest growing in the nation. Currently, some 1,300 students are seeking bachelor's and master's degrees in a variety of fields.

Bachelor's degrees are available in criminal justice, elementary education, exceptional education, general business administration, legal studies, liberal studies, nursing, psychology, and social sciences. Master's degrees are offered in business administration, criminal justice, educational leadership, engineering, exceptional education, public administration, and language arts/reading education. Local businesses especially are well served by the MBA program, which allows fully-employed students to attend classes at night or on weekends.

Live Oak Inn

(Bed & Breakfast Restaurant)

This 115-year-old house, noteworthy for its coquina foundation and rubble chimney, makes up half of the historic Live Oak Inn bed & breakfast.

Step back in time to the pioneering days of Daytona Beach at the Live Oak Inn. One of Florida's top historic bed and breakfast inns, the Live Oak stands where Daytona began.

The inn consists of two late 1800s buildings constructed by two of Daytona's earliest settlers who helped begin fulfilling Mathias Day's dream of a city of large houses and beautiful gardens.

In 1871, Riley Peck brought his family to Daytona from Albány, New York, and bought a large corner lot on Beach Street from Day. The property had been the site of Colonel Samuel Williams's plantation from 1790 until Seminole Indians burned the homestead to the ground in the 1830s.

Peck built what today is the oldest remaining five-room residence in Daytona Beach. A decade later, in 1881, he divided his lot and sold the southern portion to his brother Myron, who constructed a two-and-a-half story wood frame building, considered the oldest remaining building in the city.

The two structures at 444 and 448 South Beach Street today are connected by a breezeway. Together with a carriage house and the city's oldest remaining garden, all partly enclosed by the oldest stone wall, this is the Live Oak Inn.

The inn is owned and operated by the Rev. Delmar J. Glock and his wife, Jessie Glock, a Florida native. The Glocks purchased the property in 1979 and maintained it as their private residence for ten years. After a stint as missionaries around the world, the Glocks returned to Daytona Beach in 1994, and took on a new role as innkeepers.

Jessie Glock says the Live Oak allows guests to experience turn-of-the-century Daytona Beach, but with all the modern comforts.

Guests can choose from fifteen rooms decorated to pay tribute to events and people in Florida history. Each room has a private bath, some with Jacuzzis or Victorian soaking tubs. Most of the beds are king- or queen-sized. Some rooms include private verandas. And most overlook either the Halifax Harbor Marina on the Halifax River or the historic garden.

This 125-year-old house, part of the Live Oak Inn, is the oldest standing building in Daytona Beach. The stone wall out front is also the oldest in town.

Owner Jessie Glock enjoys the flower bed at the Live Oak Inn.

Owner Delmar Glock stands in the breezeway connecting Daytona's two oldest standing homes which make up the Live Oak Inn.

City of Daytona Beach

Above: Beach Street in downtown Daytona Beach has been reinvigorated by a new streetscape.

Below: The new Halifax Harbor Marina is popular with boaters throughout the eastern United States.

The City of Daytona Beach has one clear goal: to lead the Halifax area into a renaissance to rival the golden years of ***The World's Most Famous Beach***.

Over more than a century, through waves of boom times and bad times, the hard work and ingenuity of people like Mathias Day and Jerome Burgman and Mary McLeod Bethune enabled Daytona Beach not only to survive and prosper, but to dazzle the world.

Today, rather than wait for another towering entrepreneurial figure to lead the way, the city has embarked on a course which city planner Gerald Langston predicts could reinvigorate Daytona Beach every bit as successfully as the resurrection of South Miami Beach more than a decade ago.

Like Miami Beach, Daytona Beach, as one of Florida's oldest tourist destinations, suffered over time as visitors went looking for new experiences and newer accommodations.

To encourage private investment and reverse the downward trend, the city is spending millions of dollars to beautify public spaces and to help businesses and homeowners rehabilitate private property. The government also has put its economic and regulatory clout behind a series of public-private ventures designed to jump-start the development and redevelopment of critical areas of the city.

The transformation is evident in the downtown business district, the Main Street redevelopment area, the Halifax Harbor Marina and the Ladies Professional Golf Association headquarters and championship course.

Heading into the 21st century, Daytona Beach, a city of 63,000 people headed by a council-manager form of government, is poised for progress.

Downtown Business District

Like downtowns throughout America, Daytona's Beach Street—the center of life and commerce for a century—very nearly boarded up in the 1970s with the coming of the suburban mall.

Today, trendy restaurants and bars, specialty shops and boutiques and professional offices fill nearly every storefront on Beach Street, with more merchants on waiting lists to get in. The change occurred so swiftly and so thoroughly that even residents are startled.

Much credit goes to the city's redevelopment of its riverfront parks and the Deco-inspired $1.8 million streetscaping of South Beach Street which gave the business district a fresh, vibrant

Olympic torch runners jog down the World's Most Famous Beach. More special events are being created to draw visitors to the area.

appeal. The city added public parking lots and helped merchants create colorful new façades. The streetscaping of North Beach Street is scheduled for Spring 1997.

Halifax Harbor Marina

The largest marina on the east coast of the United States south of Baltimore opened on the Daytona Beach riverfront in 1989. The Halifax Harbor Marina, financed by the city for $12 million, includes 540 boat slips—which are near fully occupied—a two-story shopping and restaurant plaza that opened in 1993 and a public park.

The marina is adjacent to the Old Daytona Historic District and, as expected, the marina is a catalyst for redevelopment of this area. In its wake, two of Daytona's oldest buildings have been turned into a popular bed-and-breakfast inn, other historic properties are being renovated and an existing condominium is expanding. The city has landscaped, and installed unique street signs and antique lighting in the historic district.

Main Street Redevelopment Area

The pre-eminent landmark on Daytona's oceanfront is a 16-story, stair-stepped luxury hotel (now the Adam's Mark Resort) built in 1989 as a public-private venture. Along with the county's Ocean Center across the street, the hotel was the first stage in a city plan to redevelop the 278-acre core of the beachside tourist district.

Using its powers of zoning and eminent domain to advantage, the city today is encouraging developers to build more luxury accommodations adjacent to the Adam's Mark and to create a critical mass of water parks, miniature golf courses and other family amusements. New bridges connecting the mainland to the beachside are in the works north and south of the district at Seabreeze and International Speedway Boulevards.

Along with plans to streetscape Atlantic Avenue, grants to spruce up Main Street façades and work to protect and rehabilitate Surfside Village, an area of historic homes, the city is heralding a renewed commitment to tourism as Daytona prepares to enter its third millennium as an internationally known tourist destination.

Ladies Professional Golf Association

The new LPGA headquarters and championship golf course west of Interstate 95 is the culmination of a successful public-private venture to bring high-quality new development to Daytona Beach. In 1989, a tri-party plan was worked out under which a private landowner donated 558 acres and the city built an award-winning golf course and secured major road improvements including a new I-95 interchange to lure the LPGA to town.

Now Daytona is reaping the benefits. A new 4,500-acre luxury golf community of villas, million-dollar homes and resort hotels around the LPGA is under development, and the city can legitimately proclaim itself a superior golfing destination.

The city continues to put its muscle behind developers wishing to bring quality projects to Daytona. As this is being written, City Manager Carey Smith has established a streamlined permitting process for new development. Smith also has created a citizens' committee to write the city's first-ever strategic plan for economic development.

Daytona Beach is famous for family fun. The beach and river provide plenty of opportunities for fishing and watersports.

Kinsey Vincent Pyle

Above: Kinsey Vincent Pyle senior members (l-r) Richard A. Burt, S. LaRue Williams, and J. Doyle Tumbleson.

Below: Roy Kinsey, Frank Pyle and Aubrey Vincent at the law firm's first office over Pete Paul's Drug Store.

Long before the O.J. Simpson ***trial of the century*** showed millions of television viewers just how arduous the judicial process can be, the law firm of Kinsey Vincent Pyle set the record for marathon legal events.

The setting: a Daytona Beach courtroom in the 1980s. On one side, the owners of three new oceanfront motels who sued the general contractor for $25 million, claiming the buildings were falling apart. Declaring one motel unsafe, the City of Ormond Beach went so far as to evacuate guests in their bathrobes in the middle of the night.

On the other side, represented by Kinsey Vincent Pyle, the contractor, who blamed the architect and the owner.

The trial dragged on for 13 long months, pausing only for a two-week vacation and Christmas. By the time the judge ruled, the case had earned the distinction of being the longest continuous construction trial in U.S. legal history, a record that stands today.

The winner: Kinsey Vincent Pyle's client who collected $1.2 million for wrongful termination from the job.

Endurance trials such as this are rare. In fact, Kinsey Vincent Pyle settles 95 percent of its cases out of court. But the firm prides itself on having the experience and organizational skills to manage the most complex litigation.

In and out of the courtroom, the firm has demonstrated staying power. In 1996, Kinsey Vincent Pyle celebrates its 50th anniversary, and lays claim to being the oldest law firm in continuous operation in Daytona Beach.

Founded in 1946 by Roy Kinsey and Aubrey Vincent, and joined a few years later by Frank Pyle, the firm from its earliest days emphasized real estate, construction and business law and, as a result, has played a role in some of the Halifax area's most far-reaching developments.

Kinsey was one of the first lawyers to develop expertise in condominium law and drafted the legal documents used by the early oceanfront high-rises. Vincent, hired in the late 1950s by Bill France's new Daytona International Speedway Corp., helped France acquire rights to land held by the Daytona Beach Racing and Recreational Facilities District, leading to the creation of the area's top tourist attraction.

Although Kinsey, Vincent and Pyle are all deceased, the firm, now located at 150 South Palmetto Avenue in City Center East, continues under the direction of senior members S. LaRue Williams, J. Doyle Tumbleson and Richard A. Burt.

Recent high-profile cases include the firm's representation of three controversial Developments of Regional Impact: Halifax Plantation, Ormond Lake and Hunters Ridge. All are long-term, almost city-sized housing and commercial developments that won state and local permits in the late 1970s and 1980s during a period of strong no-growth sentiment throughout the state.

As a leading construction law firm in a community of projected growth, Kinsey Vincent Pyle expects continued expansion of its real estate practice representing major developers and lending institutions as well as individual buyers. Additionally, the firm continues its tradition of quality, innovative representation of business clients of all sizes and varied business activities.

Left: Businesses in the city of Daytona Beach Shores contributed half the money to erect striking new markers at the city limits.

City of Daytona Beach Shores

Markers at the city limits of Daytona Beach Shores proclaim that "Life Is Better Here." For the nearly 2,700 permanent residents of this coastal community, that's not just a motto. The combination of low taxes, quality services and beach living make Daytona Beach Shores one of the Halifax area's most attractive addresses.

One of the area's youngest cities, Daytona Beach Shores began to take shape in 1960 when a group of moteliers formed a small taxing district to pay for municipal services. They called their enclave "2,000 Cottages," a fitting name in an era when the beachfront was a collection of mom-and-pop motels.

The city was incorporated in 1967, and its contour ensured that tourism would remain the chief industry. Daytona Beach Shores is a 5.5 mile strip along the Atlantic Ocean. In some places, the city is only one block wide. Today, vintage motel cottages intermingle with new high-rise hotels and condominiums. In winter, when tourists and seasonal residents arrive, the city's population swells to nearly 16,000. During special event weeks Speedweeks, Bike Week and Spring Break - the city hosts as many as 30,000 people.

Under a council/manager form of government, Daytona Beach Shores provides a wide range of services in a cost-effective manner. The city maintains a large recreational park, two oceanfront parks, a garden park and a community center. In December, the annual Light Up the Shores festival features hundreds of lighted Christmas trees along city streets and a nighttime Christmas parade billed as the "Macy's of the South."

Plans are in the works to open a beachside museum and welcome center promoting the city's racing history. A city-commissioned survey has established the precise beginning and ending points of the famed "Measured Mile" where, in 1935, Sir Malcolm Campbell set the last land speed record (276.82) on Volusia County beaches. Permanent markers are planned at each end of the run.

After listening to residents' concerns in a community forum in 1993, Daytona Beach Shores became one of the few cities in the United States to build and operate a dedicated Emergency Operations Center which has been activated several times to assist residents as hurricanes approached.

Even though the city has enhanced its services over the past decade, it has reduced the property tax rate by 23.5 percent. Thanks to a frugal government and a 1996 tax base of $517 million, the city has one of the lowest utility rate structures, the lowest property tax rate and the lowest cost of community services in all of Volusia County. All reasons why residents call Daytona Beach Shores "A Gem on the Atlantic Ocean."

Below: The municipal offices of Daytona Beach Shores get into the spirit of Light Up the Shores, the annual holiday fesitval which features hundreds of Christmas trees and thousands of lights.

Olds Hall Good Samaritan Center

Above: Olds Hall is named for Ransom Olds, builder of the original Oldsmobile and a longtime resident of the Daytona/Ormond area. He bought the building that now houses the Olds Hall Good Samaritan Center as a retirement home for missionaries and clergymen.

Below: A 120-bed skilled nursing center was added to Olds Hall soon after the property was acquired by The Evangelical Lutheran Good Samaritan Society.

The colorful history of auto racing in the Halifax began in 1902 with a contest on the beach between Alexander Winton and Ransom Olds, the man for whom Olds Hall Good Samaritan Center is named. Olds lost the speed trial, but that hardly mattered. His "Oldsmobile," which sold for $650 in those days, was already on its way to making him a millionaire.

Like many of the wealthy industrialists who wintered in Daytona and Ormond at the turn-of-the-century, Olds wanted his winter home to benefit from his philanthropy. The mild winters and invigorating ocean air were known to extend the life of the wealthy men and women who wintered here—Olds live to be eighty-six, and John D. Rockfeller, ninety-eight. So Olds decided it would be fitting to share that environment with retired missionaries and ministers of all faiths, men and women who had devoted the best years of their lives to helping others, but in their retirement years had little in the way of savings. He founded Olds Hall as a retirement home for them.

The property at 340 S. Ridgewood Avenue had once been a hotel built by Julian Arroya, a Venezuelan jurist who had immigrated to the United States at the turn-of-the-century and later practiced law with Franklin Roosevelt and Henry Stimson. The Arroya Gardens Hotel opened in the early 1920s. When Olds purchased it in 1942 and created the retirement home, which has been referred to as the "house of contentment."

The Evangelical Lutheran Good Samaritan Society, the nation's largest non-profit provider of long-term care for the elderly, purchased Olds Hall in 1972. A nursing center was added in 1974 and expanded in 1976. Today it serves as a multi-level retirement community, offering independent living, assisted living, and nursing care with a Christian focus. Today, the Society is raising funds to open an Alzheimer's unit and rehabilitation room.

The nursing center has 120 beds and is rated superior by the Florida Agency for Healthcare Administration. There are thirty-four apartments for assisted living, and forty-one one-bedroom, two-bedroom, and efficiency apartments for independent living. The 150 employees and 70 volunteers work to give residents the very finest in care and accommodations. Olds Hall is a part of The Evangelical Lutheran Church of America's social ministry. It is not owned or operated by the church, and the center itself is interdenominational.

Ransom Olds and his wife, Metta, always took a personal interest in Olds Hall, visiting often and frequently joining residents in Sunday evening services.

"I can assure you," Olds once wrote to Francis Tucker, then president of the Olds Hall Fellowship, "I have never done anything that has given me greater satisfaction than supplying a home for such worthy people . . . ."

That same satisfaction in the care they give motivates the employees and volunteers at Olds Hall today.

Haigh-Black Funeral Home

Evelyn Brooks
(1879-1948)

Audrey Brooks Haigh
(1905-1978)

J. Harry Haigh
(1900-1977)

Many of Daytona's most important businesses can trace their roots to the beach, but perhaps none has a more unlikely, or romantic, connection than the Haigh-Black Funeral Home.

It was 1922 when Evelyn Brooks and her daughter, Audrey, stopped to visit friends in Daytona Beach enroute to Miami. Audrey was invited to a beach party, where she met some intriguing young people, including Harry Haigh. She was so enchanted with the beach and her new friends that she persuaded her mother to stay.

Except for a quick trip back to Buffalo, New York, to sell Evelyn's interest in the family funeral home business there, the Brooks never left. In 1924, Audrey married Harry who had been elected city clerk of the then-town of Seabreeze, serving simultaneously as city assessor, a sergeant in the police department, building and plumbing inspector, and chief of the fire department.

Four years later, Evelyn Brooks was visiting in Central Florida and saw a *for sale* sign on a funeral home. She promptly purchased all the equipment and went into business in Daytona Beach with her son in law.

Haigh-Brooks Morticians opened in January 1931 in a storefront on Main Street next to Pinewood Cemetery. Three years later, the funeral home and the family, which now included a daughter, Joanne, moved into a three-bedroom house on Broadway. This was a time of "juggling." Two bedrooms served as casket selection rooms, the breakfast room doubled as an office and family room for relatives of the deceased, and the living room became a chapel. Joanne remembers one Christmas when a series of funerals necessitated moving the fully decorated Christmas tree out of the living room and into the hall three times before the family gave up and dismantled it.

On January 1, 1940, Haigh-Brooks moved to its present location at 103 E. International Speedway Boulevard (then called Broadway).

Audrey became a full partner in the business in 1948 when her mother died. The same year, Joanne married Robert H. Black. The newlyweds attended mortuary college together and became partners in the firm in 1954. This partnership necessitated a name change to the Haigh-Black Funeral Home. Joanne Haigh Black took her first death call at age eight. In 1970, she became one of the first women in Florida to become a licensed funeral director.

Following the death of her parents and husband, Joanne welcomed one of her sons, Norman, into the firm.

Both the Haigh and Black families were Daytona pioneers. Harry Haigh was the son of Catherine and Sydney Haigh, who made their home in Seabreeze in 1896. Robert Black was the son of Sarah and Harry Black, who were winter residents starting in 1905, becoming permanent residents a few years later.

Joanne and Norman continue the family tradition, now in its fourth generation, in what Joanne calls a true ministry of helping people in their time of loss.

Joanne Haigh Black

Norman Black

Robert H. Black
(1902-1985)

Dr. Carl Lentz, whose ancestors came to Daytona Beach in the 1800s, has practiced medicine here since 1979.

Carl W. Lentz, III, M.D., F.A.C.S. Plastic Surgeon

Dr. Carl W. Lentz, III, a plastic surgeon who has practiced in Daytona Beach since 1979, can claim a rare local heritage: his great grandparents, Laurence and Mary Eliza Thompson, came to Daytona in 1875 with Mathias Day, just a year after Day bought up the old Samuel Williams plantation and began to lay out the city of his dreams. The Thompsons made their way from Cincinnati, Ohio, by train and steamboat. There were only ten families in Daytona at the time.

Laurence Thompson was to become one of the new city's most prominent men. He and his brother Graham ran a dry goods store, Thompson Brothers, located next door to his home on Beach Street. Later he sold the store, helping first to found the Equitable Building and Loan Company and then establishing the first real estate and insurance business in town. He was among the twenty-six men who voted on incorporation in 1876, became the first town clerk and served on the Town Council.

In 1887, Thompson bought land on Beach Street between Orange Avenue and Cottage Lane, where he established an orange grove and three stores, with public rooms above that served as a city auditorium and opera house. His gift of the riparian rights from the riverfront property resulted in the formation of the Halifax River Yacht Club. Also, part of his beachside property on Silver Beach was donated for construction of one of several bridges connecting the peninsula to the mainland.

His son, also Laurence Thompson, (there was an older sister Lillian and younger brother Harry as well) eventually took over the family business. He served as a director of the Florida Bank and Trust Company (now First Union Bank) and was on the Board of Trustees of Bethune-Cookman College. Dr. Lentz is the son of this Laurence Thompson's daughter, Kay, who married a career army officer named Carl Lentz. His father was overseas during World War II when Dr. Lentz was born in Daytona Beach. And although the family would for many years move from one army base to another, Dr. Lentz's mother always liked to return to her hometown and her family. When his father retired, Dr. Lentz's parents moved to Daytona Beach permanently.

While a student at Seabreeze High School in Daytona Beach, Dr. Lentz was introduced to the excitement of the study of medicine by his Godfather, Dr. P.A. Drohomer, a local general surgeon. Naturally, he gravitated toward the practice of surgery. After receiving his undergraduate degree from Emory University, a medical degree from the University of Miami and completing five years of general surgery residency at Keesler USAF Medical Center, he elected to study the art of medicine: plastic surgery. He came to realize that form follows function. During the subsequent two-year plastic surgery residency at Wilford Hall USAF Medical Center, he studied the theory of surgery and learned to rebuild those who were victims of birth defects, accidents, injuries, the ravages of cancer, other illnesses and the aging process. Through his training, he developed a belief that it was not only the quantity of life that was important but also the quality. He has worked to master the techniques that restore physical health as well as the patient's body image. He and his staff feel that each patient is special with specific concerns. They have committed themselves to patient care, and have made a concerted effort to relieve patients' suffering and fears by their individual efforts and by their work with other local and national health care providers. Dr. Lentz believes complete health care of the highest quality is available in Volusia County. Through the use of the highest quality local physicians, patients can be assured that their health care needs can be met locally or that they will be referred to the appropriate care elsewhere in the nation.

As Dr. Lentz's great-grandfather supported the arts, he has helped establish the Florida International Festival which brings the London Symphony Orchestra to Daytona bi-annually. As did his grandfather, Dr. Lentz serves on the board of First Union Bank, previously known as Florida National Bank. As a doctor, he has been active in his professional societies. He has served as president of the Volusia County Medical Society and is chairman of the Florida Medical Association's committee on national legislative affairs. He has served as president of the Florida Society of Plastic and Reconstructive Surgeons, chairman of the Department of Surgery at Halifax Medical Center and chief of plastic surgery at Halifax, Ormond Memorial Hospital-Daytona Beach and Daytona Community, now known as Columbia.

In the tradition of his father, a West Point graduate, Dr. Lentz also served his country and completed 13 years of active duty with the United States Air Force, leaving the service as a lieutenant colonel, consultant to the Surgeon General. He spent 13 years as a reservist for the United States Army and retired as a full colonel after 26 years of total service. His last assignment was commander of the 567th Maxillofacial Reconstructive Unit which he led into deployment to Saudi Arabia, Desert Storm and Desert Shield.

It is fitting that a local boy, born in Daytona, raised as an army brat throughout the world, inspired by great doctors and great community sponsors would return to Daytona and work hard as a plastic surgeon still contributing to the social, professional, political and individual needs of the community. With his heritage, he hopes to continue the tradition of service.

The old Thompson Brothers store and home on Beach Street were built by ancestors of Lentz. The store building, although altered, still stands.

Black Crow Broadcasting

Black Crow Broadcasting's studio at 126 W. International Speedway Boulevard became an instant landmark in downtown Daytona Beach.

Black Crow Broadcasting first signed on the air in May 1995, so the fledgling company is just starting to write its own chapter in the history of the Daytona Beach/Halifax area. But the company speaks volumes about the direction in which the community is heading and the possibilities for the future.

Two years ago, Mike Linn, then working at his father's radio station in Fort Myers, struck out on his own. Driving around Florida in search of an opportunity, Linn and his wife, Nicole, found what they were looking for in Daytona Beach.

Here, the Linns discovered a big radio market—the 95th largest in the nation—with little competition on the FM dial. They also found an FM station, WEDG in Edgewater, up for sale.

At the time, WEDG broadcasted an oldies format pulled off a satellite, while the area's two major FM competitors played country or adult contemporary music. Rock -'n'- roll fans had to tune into Orlando stations.

Changing both the call letters and the format, Black Crow debuted as WKRO, 93.1-FM, an alternative music station targeting a young, Generation-X crowd. The formula worked. In 18 months, Linn says, revenue jumped tenfold.

If the Black Crow story ended here, the moral might be that the Halifax area is fertile ground for entrepreneurs with new ideas and money to spend.

But there's more to Black Crow's investment.

Deciding that their station, operating out of a double-wide trailer in Edgewater, needed a higher profile in the community, the Linns headed to downtown Daytona Beach where they found real estate very affordable. They purchased the historic Commercial Bank building at 126 W. International Speedway Boulevard for $125,000 and put $168,000 into renovations. Adorned with the striking KRO logo, the building immediately became a new landmark, prompting city officials to plan an expansion of the historic district to take in the property.

Feeling confident about the future of the Daytona Beach/Halifax area, the Linns in the summer of 1996 added two more local stations to Black Crow's portfolio: WNDB-AM, a popular talk radio outlet, and its FM affiliate, WTSM. And, to accommodate their acquisitions, they bought an adjacent building and warehouse.

For a young company, Black Crow is making a big impact.

Mike Linn, who grew up around radio stations, spent two years practicing law before following in his father's footsteps. After joining the family business, Nicole went on hiatus for a few years to research and write a book on radio promotions. She serves as Black Crow's marketing director.

Promotions have played a big part in the company's success. The KRO call letters were selected in part to appeal subliminally to a young crowd already listening to the alternative rock band Counting Crows and singer Sheryl Crow. The station announced its arrival by playing Pizzicato 5's "Twiggy Twiggy" for 62 hours straight, until police were called out to investigate.

The company employs what it calls the KRO Krew: 12 young men and women dressed in special KRO outfits who appear at remote broadcasts, mingle with the fans and serve as what Nicole calls "lifestyle ambassadors." For the diehard listeners who venture downtown to the Black Crow building, a street-level boutique sells clothes designed to appeal to a hip Gen-X crowd.

The company's newest acquisitions are getting some of the same promotional treatment. WTSM was changed to WHOG, which is being marketed to an older and more male crowd. In selecting the call letters, the reverence for customized Harley Davidson motorcycles in Daytona Beach was not lost on the Linns.

As this is being written, no major changes are planned for WNDB's talk and news format.

Mike Linn doesn't rule out further radio and real estate acquisitions. After nearly two years, he's convinced of the opportunities for growth and profit in the Daytona Beach/ Halifax area.

The Linns and Black Crow Broadcasting represent part of the renaissance underway in Daytona Beach. A city on the move once more and an energetic new company - each offering something to the other.

Black Crow operates three radio stations—WKRO, WNDB and WHOG—all with a primary market of Volusia and Flagler Counties.

El Caribe Motel

Above: The El Caribe opened a new tower and conference room in 1991 while still maintaining the charm of old Florida hospitality. The addition includes a 3,000 square foot oceanfront meeting room.

Below: Neon hot air balloons light the way for guests at the El Caribe Resort and Conference Center.

The search for the grave of Mary Ann Richardson's great-great-grandmother came to a dead end at the Office of the Registrar in Edinburgh, Scotland. All inquiries of the little graveyards that dot the countryside brought the same response: *no trace found.*

But on the last day of a family pilgrimage to their ancestral home, something in Mary Ann's gut told her to go to the village of Lilliesleaf. There, behind the Church of Scotland, beyond the first rows of headstones, through an old gate, two headstones down, Mary Ann found what she and her parents had come for.

And for a moment, Mary Ann and her mother, Rosemary, must have gazed upon the grave of this long-dead proprietress of a temperance house—an inn that served no alcohol—and wondered whether it was by divine plan, or because of something in the blood, or by sheer coincidence that each of these three women—mother, daughter, and great-great-grandmother—had traveled the same road.

Mary Ann Richardson has operated the El Caribe Resort at 2125 South Atlantic Avenue in Daytona Beach Shores since 1976. Rosemary Richardson ran the motel for the fifteen years prior to that. Neither woman had ever expected to follow their ancestor into the innkeeping business, but Mary Ann has a feeling that this was meant to be.

It surely didn't seem so thirty-five years ago when the El Caribe was acquired by the Richardsons.

In 1961, the Richardsons were living in Jackson, Tennessee, and betting their future on automotive parts.

H. A. "Rich" Richardson, Mary Ann's father and Rosemary's husband, had anticipated that GIs returning from World War II would be buying cars in record numbers. And those cars no doubt would break down. So he started an auto parts business, called Motor Parts & Bearings Company, to meet the demand that was sure to come.

Over the years, the business grew to almost fifty stores and a warehouse in three states, thanks in part to a WATTS line that enabled him to make unlimited long-distance telephone calls for one price.

Rich Richardson's WATTS line happened to be the first one in Jackson. And it made him a popular man in town, with friends and customers dropping by the shop after hours to use the phone. One day, a man who came by to use the phone invited Rich Richardson to invest in a Florida motel with him and his brother.

Rich Richardson saw not destiny but a good business deal in the El Caribe Motel. But six months later, with the motel teetering on bankruptcy, Richardson took over the motel from his partners, and fate began to take its course.

Ask Rosemary Richardson how she—a quiet, gracious housewife and mother of five children, who had never set foot in Florida—came to run a fifty-two-unit motel in Daytona Beach Shores, and she'll tell you: *Rich told me to do it.*

Rich Richardson was not the type of man to sell off anything once acquired; Rosemary was not the type of woman to contradict her hus-

Left: After operating the El Caribe for 15 years, Rosemary and H. A. "Rich" Richardson enjoy year-round retirement in Daytona Beach Shores.

band. And so Rosemary began living her double life: Southern wife and mother in Tennessee from fall through spring, and savvy Florida businesswoman come summer tourist season.

Rosemary remembers the years of loading up the car with her summer gear and at least one of her children, and heading south to Daytona Beach Shores as happy ones. The work was hard—guests vividly recall seeing her out sweeping the pool deck every morning at 7:00—but at least it left little time to wallow in homesickness. Mary Ann, the oldest of the Richardson children, will never forget her mother rousting her out late in the evening to clean a just-vacated room so it could be rented again that night.

With no business inclination herself, Mary Ann was on her way to becoming a professional student. But after seven years of graduate school, Rich Richardson decided enough was enough, and in 1976 told his daughter: *Go earn a living.*

With Rich Richardson's health beginning to fail, the Richardsons were only too happy to turn over the El Caribe to Mary Ann.

Three years into the business, Mary Ann decided she wanted to expand by building a tower on an adjacent beachfront lot. Calling her father to get his blessing, Rich Richardson told his daughter: *Do it.*

Left to her own devices, Mary Ann, who would become the only female president ever of the Florida Hotel & Motel Association, not only figured out how to build a motel building, she figured out how to fill it. And the solution she came up with is what still sets the Christian tone for the El Caribe today.

The tower opened in 1979 in time for successful race weeks, but by August, Mary Ann was facing a disastrous fall season with only one reservation: a visiting minister booked by the pastor of Mary Ann's own church. Long a quietly religious woman, Mary Ann began to pray, and soon her inspiration came.

Writing to churches throughout Florida and promoting the El Caribe for church retreats, Mary Ann soon filled up the tower. Today, church and ministry groups remain her bread-and-butter.

Below: Rosemary Richardson (right) turns control of the resort over to Mary Ann (left). The close mother-daughter relationship is captured in this portrait.

Sun Viking Lodge

A family tradition began in 1953 when Karl and Carrie Evensgaard became proprietors of the Ocean Villa Motel.

The popularity of the Sun Viking Lodge today reflects more than four decades of experience in the hotel industry by the Browns and Evensgaards.

The prestigious "Hotelier of the Year" award of the Florida Hotel and Motel Association goes to men and women who think big, and have the accomplishments to prove it.. That usually means big hotels, the latest trends and plenty of self-promotion. Usually, it doesn't mean someone like Gary Brown, the 1994 Hotelier of the Year, whose old-fashioned ideas of hospitality include coloring books for kids and, at Christmas, a tree in every room.

Gary and Barbara Brown were still newlyweds when they bought their first beachside motel in 1971. With the help of Barbara's parents, Karl and Carrie Evensgaard, they took over the tiny eleven-unit Oceanfront Villas in Daytona Beach Shores. They worked every day for two years without a day off. It was a struggle, especially with the addition of two children, Karla and Gregory.

But on their side the Browns had what they like to call the Norwegian hospitality genes. Barbara's parents were well-established Daytona Beach hoteliers. Her father, Karl, was a former Norwegian Naval officer who crossed the Atlantic many times during World War II and once survived four days at sea in a life raft, and her mother, Carrie, was an Italian immigrant. The Evensgaards acquired their first motel, the Ocean Villa, in 1953, after visiting and falling in love with the beach. They worked hard, and over the years added two more properties: the Capri Motel and the Casa Marina Motel.

In 1978, the Browns took the plunge and demolished the aging Oceanfront Villas. In its place they built the forty-unit Sun Viking Lodge, a nod to Barbara's Norwegian heritage. Again in 1986, with the purchase of the adjoining property, an opportunity arose to build an eight-story addition expanding to 91 units. Currently, the Sun Viking Lodge is a first class oceanfront resort offering one of the highest quality ratings in the Daytona Beach area.

Just as the first two generations became involved with the motel business, Gary's and Barbara's two children have worked in the family operations since their early years. Karla graduated from Florida State University with a Hospitality degree in Hotel/Restaurant Administration. She works at the Walt Disney World Dolphin Hotel as a manager and plans to return to the family business in the future and take over the operations that her parents and grandparents have developed. Gregory graduated from Southern Methodist University with a degree in Cinema and hopes to pursue a career in the motion picture industry. However, everyone expects that the Norwegian hospitality genes may some day surface and he too will join the family business.

The Browns eagerly concentrate on family vacationers who have always been the backbone of the Sun Viking's clientele: the sixty-foot waterslide, the largest kiddie playground on the beach and lots of year-round family activities add to the ***Families Welcome*** atmosphere.

Gary Brown is not short on the kind of innovations that come with being Hotelier of the Year, however. He has been a leader in getting hotels to think bigger and act in unison. And his ideas, such as uniting hotels and golf courses to promote Daytona as a golfing destination, have been profitable, often as much for other hoteliers as for himself.

Bethune Cookman College

History-rich Bethune-Cookman College has for nearly a century made contributions to the Halifax Area. In an effort to develop long-lasting relationships with the Daytona Beach community, Dr. Mary McLeod Bethune's legacy of "friend-raising" would continue for many years and make Bethune-Cookman College the first and oldest four-year college in Daytona Beach.

The fifteenth child of former slaves, Dr. Mary McLeod Bethune, Bethune-Cookman's founder, was born in 1875. Dr. Bethune moved to Daytona Beach and, in 1904, founded the Daytona Literary and Industrial School for Training Negro Girls, therefore implementing her dream of establishing a school which would educate and train children of freed slaves and railroad workers. The school site was a trash dump west of the railroad tracks, and Dr. Bethune's only assets were $1.50, faith in God, and five little girls.

Through her persistent efforts, Dr. Bethune realized that wealthy women residing in Daytona Beach during the winter could be organized to "shepherd" the well-being of her school. Known as the Women's Advisory Board, they furnished the living quarters for the girls and later the infirmary. The group's best known and most lasting effort is the Women's Advisory Annual Bazaar, first held in 1911. Cynthia Ranslow, whose husband founded the local liberal nondenominational Tourist Church, served as first president of the Advisory Board.

By 1915, Dr. Bethune had assembled an impressive list of philanthropists, including James Gamble of the Proctor and Gamble Company of Cincinnati. Gamble later agreed to be the first president of the school's Trustee Board. Thomas White, president of White Sewing Machine Company, also a member of the board, lobbied the City Council to provide electricity and water for the school and contributed to the McLeod Hospital, and Faith Hall. White, before his death in 1914, left the school $79,000. Therefore, in tribute to his generosity, White Hall, the school's first brick structure and administrative building, was dedicated.

At the urging of Gamble and seen as an opportunity to expand her dream of educating all children, Dr. Bethune's school became a coeducational institution in 1923, with the merger of Daytona Normal and Industrial Institute and Cookman Institute of Jacksonville.

In 1942, following her retirement as president, Dr. Bethune hand-picked her successor, James Colston, who wanted to take the school in an exclusively academic direction and away from its vocational roots. Unable to bring such to realization, Colston resigned in 1946, just before reaching the final stages of the regional accreditation process for Bethune-Cookman College. Following was Dr. Richard V. Moore, whose term can be easily noted as one of the College's most important eras. Dr. Moore continued the thrust of Dr. Colston's academic emphasis while leaving Dr. Bethune's vocational programs untouched, until 1955, the year of Dr. Bethune's death. Moore expanded the curriculum to social sciences, business and hard sciences and was a highly successful fund raiser, increasing the school's endowment by $6 million.

One of the most effective community volunteer groups was the Board of Counselors. At the suggestion of J. Saxon Lloyd, a trustee and local business leader, Dr. Moore developed the community group to promote the educational, religious and financial interests of the College. Lloyd, Pat Murphy, and James Kilborne, together suggested that the Board of Counselors be a committee including diverse gender and race. The Counselors sponsor such activities as an annual reception to introduce and welcome new faculty and staff members to the Daytona Beach leadership and Halifax community. The Board of Counselors goals today remain the same.

Since 1975, the College has endured enormous growth under the current president, Dr. Oswald P. Bronson, Sr., who has increased the College's offerings to 37 majors in business, education, science and mathematics, social sciences and humanities, secured $35 million for renovations and construction to expand the campus to 33 buildings on 60 acres, and increased the College's endowment to $17 million. Today, Bethune-Cookman College, a renown, historically black, liberal arts, United Methodist church-related institution, operates a budget that exceeds $34 million. With a diversified faculty and staff of 400 and a diversified student body of more than 2,300, the College makes a $212 million impact on the Halifax Area economy. Recently, the College embarked upon a $25 million capital campaign for endowment and construction, its most ambitious fund raising effort ever.

For more information, contact the Bethune-Cookman College Office of Public Relations at (904) 253-5172.

Above: James N. Gamble of Proctor & Gamble was one of the wealthy visitors to Daytona Beach won over by Mary McLeod Bethune's vision. Gamble became one of Bethune's staunchest supporters, serving in 1905 as the first president of the school's board of trustees.

Below: Students at Bethune-Cookman College, known for teaching professional skills in an academically challenging environment, are recruited by corporations from Daytona Beach and around the country.

St. Paul Catholic Church

Right: Bishop Patrick Barry blessed the new St. Paul Catholic Church in 1927.

The Ku Klux Klan paraded down Beach Street in full white-hooded regalia in 1923, the year Father William Mullally arrived to take over the tiny Daytona Beach parish.

At that time, Catholics were scarce in Florida generally and in Daytona in particular, but the bigots were in their glory days. From elected officials to lowly utility workers, the city was so in the grip of the KKK that when a new Catholic family arrived in town and asked a policeman for directions to the Catholic church, they were told there was none, even though the church was only a couple blocks away.

Above: In recent renovations, marble from the old altar was used to create a new baptismal front.

Mullally, already planning to build a new house of worship, determined to do what was in his power to stop such shameful behavior. The new Catholic church, he decided, would be a Daytona landmark visible on the skyline from any point in the city, so big and tall that it could not be missed by travelers crossing the bridges "so no one could make a liar out of himself by saying there wasn't a Catholic church here."

True to Mullally's word, the new St. Paul Church—a Gothic cruciform 181 feet long, 80 feet wide, and 123 feet tall, as grand and imposing as St. Patrick's Cathedral in New York City, and capped by a Byzantine cupola and a cross of copper visible for miles—dominated the cityscape when it opened on Christmas Day 1926.

Then, as today, St. Paul Church was revered as one of the finest examples of religious architecture in Florida.

But as majestic as St. Paul was at completion, the very idea of such a church left parishioners breathless even before ground was broken in 1926. And for good reason.

The Daytona Beach parish numbered only 277 members, including 40 young children; this cathedral-like behemoth was being designed for 1,200 people. Few could envision a day when the Catholic community in Daytona Beach could support such a structure.

Catholicism in modern Florida was still in its infancy. Until 1828, there was not even one priest assigned full-time to Florida.

On June 1, 1881, Alexander and Rosena Achstetter and their children, immigrants from Germany, became the first Catholic family to move to Daytona, setting up housekeeping in a log cabin. When daughter Marie Anna got married on March 16, 1882, to George Dittman, the family had to summon Father (later Bishop) William Kenny, who rode into town by wagon from Palatka to officiate.

For several years thereafter, mass was only offered in Daytona twice a year, with services held at the old Palmetto House or at someone's home around a kitchen table.

It wasn't until 1886 that Daytona got its own priest, or at least one to share, when Father John O'Boyle was assigned to Titusville and a territory stretching from St. Augustine to West Palm Beach. He made rounds by mail boat, stopping at mail stations to celebrate mass for the few Catholics who would be waiting for him before moving down river.

Some of O'Boyle's biggest crowds were in Daytona in winter when laborers working on the Ormond Hotel and Irish immigrants who staffed the finished rooms would crowd into Sunday mass. Anticipating growth in the area, O'Boyle moved to Daytona and began holding services every Sunday in the old opera house or the armory.

O'Boyle erected Daytona's first Catholic church, a wood frame building on a corner lot at

Left: Bishop Norbert Dorsey dedicated the church during a ceremony on January 25, 1996. Father Robert Webster (left) is pastor of the church.

Below: St. Paul Catholic Church today remains one of the finest examples of church architecture in Florida.

South Palmetto and Myrtle Avenues. When it opened in 1899, the parish numbered about fifty members year-round.

The little church lasted nearly a quarter of a century. In 1923, two months after O'Boyle retired at age eighty-six, his successor, Mullally, paid $40,000 for a city block on North Ridgewood Avenue and began his grand plans for the new St. Paul Church.

The construction cost was $250,000—almost $1,000 for each man, woman, and child in the congregation—with stained glass windows and furnishings driving that cost even higher. Mullally himself wondered whether the small parish would fall into bankruptcy under the weight of this debt.

But St. Paul survived. Monsignor Mullally was succeeded as pastor by Father Thomas Gross, Father Matthew Connolly, Father Sean Heslin, and Father Fred Ruse. Today, the church—2,200 families strong—is headed by Father Robert E. Webster.

Today, after nearly seven decades, St. Paul is still the home parish for some of Daytona's leading citizens. But as many families moved to the suburbs, it has become increasingly an inner city parish, responsible for ministering to the poor, the hospitalized, and the imprisoned.

Finding inspiration in Pope John XXIII's declaration that "we are not on earth to guard a museum but to cultivate a flourishing garden of life," Webster, who lead the church's latest renovation, sees St. Paul as a beacon of new and eternal life in the city of Daytona Beach.

Daytona Beach International Airport

Above: Passengers arrive at the spacious new 166,000 square foot terminal at Daytona Beach International Airport.

Below: A bird's eye view of Daytona Beach International Airport shows the new 10,500-foot-long runway designed to accommodate international flights.

In the early days of aviation, Daytona Beach's swankier hotels would hire daredevil pilots to fly over the beach and land their planes on the hard sand. It was all for the entertainment of their wealthy winter guests, but it also made the beach itself the first airport in Volusia County. Soon, a Pitcairn Airwing was making regular airmail deliveries on the beach.

That worked well until 1928, when the city moved the airport to Bethune Point. The mail plane was still a Pitcairn Airwing and the company was Eastern Air Transport, a forerunner of Eastern Airlines. Hundreds of people turned out to watch the first airmail flight take off, only to see their mail end up in the Halifax River when the pilot couldn't make it off the short runway.

Two years later, the city moved its airport again to its present site. There wasn't much of a budget during the Depression, so the first sign was carved into an old wooden surfboard and planted in the ground. The runways were made with coquina rock.

But the airport grew . . . in more ways than one. In 1940, the city contracted a zoo keeper to run the airport. He decided to bring his menagerie along, and when the city tried to break the lease, he threatened to turn his lions loose. By this time, the DC-3 had come to Daytona Beach, and New York City was just ten hours away.

The U.S. Navy took over the airport for pilot training during World War II. After its return to city hands in 1946, plane travel began to replace rail travel as the favored mode of transportation. Not only was Daytona Beach's tourist economy boosted by the air access, but the airport became an important service for all of Volusia County. With that in mind, the county took over operation of the municipal airport in 1969 and renamed it the Daytona Beach Regional Airport.

By 1992, the airport's latest transformation to the Daytona Beach International Airport was underway. A new 166,000-square-foot terminal was opened; this was nearly three times the size of the old terminal. U.S. Customs opened an office and the airport was designated part of the county's Foreign Trade Zone, followed in 1994 by the opening of an international terminal and a newly extended 10,500-foot runway to accommodate larger planes. Finally, on November 2, 1995, an LTU International Airways passenger jet from Germany became the airport's first scheduled international flight.

Today, the airport is in the process of acquiring 850 acres south of its location for use in future aviation and commercial development.

Volusia Construction Company

At age twelve, Ronnie Bledsoe's dream was to own a backhoe. When his father, J. C. Bledsoe bought him a boat, Ronnie traded it for a down payment on his dream equipment. To pay off the machine, he rented it for $400 a month to his father's underground utilities company.

The venture was a modest success.

Twelve years later, in 1974, father and son teamed up again on a slightly larger scale. With one used tractor backhoe that Ronnie had acquired, and one dump truck, J. C. and Ronnie went into business in South Daytona as Volusia Construction Company.

This time, the payoff was substantial. Within three years, Volusia Construction earned the distinction, which it retains today, of being the largest underground utilities contractor in Volusia County.

Volusia Construction has built water, sewer, and drainage systems for the cities of Port Orange, Daytona Beach, and Ormond Beach, the community of Palm Coast, and the Daytona Beach International Airport. One of the company's biggest jobs: a $3.8 million contract with the city of Cocoa.

The company's reputation for speed and skill comes naturally.

As early as age four, when Ronnie took his first solo—and unauthorized—bulldozer ride (digging up the family's backyard), there was little doubt that he would follow in his father's footsteps.

J. C. Bledsoe owned or worked for underground utilities companies his entire career. Ronnie recalls an early affinity for heavy equipment and the feeling of accomplishment from taking a dirt field, dredging it up, and making something out of it. Growing up in Greenville, South Carolina, Ronnie took to spending every day after school and weekends on his father's job sites.

In 1970, father and son moved to the Halifax area. Four years later, with the United States mired in recession and many companies—including many local underground utilities contractors—sliding into bankruptcy, J. C. and Ronnie saw their chance to go into business for themselves.

Ronnie, then only twenty-four, was president, while his father, who had all the experience, was vice president. J. C. was looking forward to retirement, Ronnie recalls, so he "let me make all the decisions and he kept me out of trouble."

The father taught the son well. In twenty-two years, Volusia Construction grew from four employees to 80, and acquired all the backhoes a man could want.

Above: Ronnie Bledsoe built his company into Volusia County's largest underground utilities contractor.

Below: J. C. Bledsoe stirred his son's interest in construction and helped launch him in the business.

HRH Insurance

Above: HRH Insurance serves customers from its office at 115 N. Ridgewood Avenue.

HRH Insurance is the oldest agency in Daytona Beach but prides itself on being the most technologically advanced. The company that was founded in 1920 downtown on Beach Street is doing business in new and creative ways. They view increased technology as the vehicle to provide more efficient service to their clients.

HRH began as a sole proprietorship by Guy B. Odum and was incorporated in 1946 when King Bishop joined the firm. By 1958, a nephew, Jay Adams, joined Guy B. Odum & Company. Over a period of years, Adams purchased the firm and changed the name to Jay Adams & Associates in 1976.

The final change came in 1986 when the agency was acquired by a national brokerage, Hilb, Rogal and Hamilton Company, a network of fifty-four offices in sixteen states. With 1995 revenues of $148 million, HRH was the tenth largest broker in the United States and the eighteenth largest in the world.

HRH of Daytona Beach is a wholly-owned subsidiary headed by president and chief executive officer Glenn Vincent. Former owner Adams remains chairman of the board and executive vice president of the holding company overseeing the Florida operations.

HRH is a full service agency, offering many types of insurance including personal, and commercial and property and casualty, workers compensation, marine, aviation, employee benefits and other specialty coverages. Additional services provided to their clients include claims administration, risk management and loss control.

Vincent, who has been with the agency since 1980, says one of the biggest changes in the business has been the increasing use of technology. In 1996, HRH went on-line with its own home page. Six employees already telecommute to work. And Vincent expects that, within the next few years, the agency will transact much of its business with customers over the Internet.

The human touch—personal relationships with its customers and personal involvement in the community—will always be first.

HRH employs thirty-seven people in Daytona Beach, and all are encouraged to take an active role in civic affairs. The agency prides itself on being one of the highest per capita contributors to the United Way's annual fundraising drives. Employees also are active in cultural and educational organizations, such as Embry Riddle Aeronautical University, Seaside Music Theater, Literacy Council, Museum of Arts & Sciences, Florida International Festival, Junior League of Daytona Beach and in such business development groups as the Chamber of Commerce and the Volusia Visions planning group.